W9-AUE-003

Adam Sandler

Titles in the People in the News series include:

Ben Affleck
Tim Allen
Drew Barrymore
Tony Blair
Bono
Garth Brooks
Sandra Bullock
George W. Bush
Nicolas Cage
Jim Carrey
Michael Crichton
Tom Cruise
Matt Damon
Johnny Depp
Celine Dion
Eminem
Michael J. Fox
Bill Gates
Mel Gibson
John Grisham
Tom Hanks
Jesse Jackson
Michael Jackson
Michael Jordan
Stephen King
Jennifer Lopez
George Lucas
Madonna
Dominique Moceanu
Rosie O'Donnell
The Osbournes
Brad Pitt
Colin Powell
Princess Diana
Prince William
Christopher Reeve
Julia Roberts
The Rolling Stones
J.K. Rowling
Arnold Schwarzenegger
Will Smith
Britney Spears
Steven Spielberg
R.L. Stine
Sting
John Travolta
Jesse Ventura
Robin Williams
Oprah Winfrey
Reese Witherspoon
Elijah Wood
Tiger Woods

PEOPLE IN THE NEWS

Adam Sandler

by Dwayne Epstein

San Diego • Detroit • New York • San Francisco • Cleveland
New Haven, Conn. • Waterville, Maine • London • Munich

For more information, contact
Lucent Books
27500 Drake Rd.
Farmington Hills, MI 48331-3535
Or you can visit our Internet site at http://www.gale.com

LIBRARY OF CONGRESS CATALOGING-IN-PUBLICATION DATA

Epstein, Dwayne.
Adam Sandler / by Dwayne Epstein.
p. cm. — (People in the news)
Summary: Describes the private life and professional career of actor-comedian Adam Sandler, who achieved popularity on the *Saturday Night Live* series.
ISBN 1-59018-447-5 (alk. paper)
1. Sandler, Adam—Juvenile literature. 2. Actors—United States—Biography—Juvenile literature. [1. Sandler, Adam. 2. Comedians. 3. Actors and actresses.] I. Title. II. People in the news (San Diego, CA.)
PN2287.S275E67 2004
791.43.028092—dc22

2003018307

Printed in the United States of America

Table of Contents

Foreword

FAME AND CELEBRITY are alluring. People are drawn to those who walk in fame's spotlight, whether they are known for great accomplishments or for notorious deeds. The lives of the famous pique public interest and attract attention, perhaps because their experiences seem in some ways so different from, yet in other ways so similar to, our own.

Newspapers, magazines, and television regularly capitalize on this fascination with celebrity by running profiles of famous people. For example, television programs such as *Entertainment Tonight* devote all of their programming to stories about entertainment and entertainers. Magazines such as *People* fill their pages with stories of the private lives of famous people. Even newspapers, newsmagazines, and television news frequently delve into the lives of well-known personalities. Despite the number of articles and programs, few provide more than a superficial glimpse at their subjects.

Lucent's People in the News series offers young readers a deeper look into the lives of today's newsmakers, the influences that have shaped them, and the impact they have had in their fields of endeavor and on other people's lives. The subjects of the series hail from many disciplines and walks of life. They include authors, musicians, athletes, political leaders, entertainers, entrepreneurs, and others who have made a mark on modern life and who, in many cases, will continue to do so for years to come.

These biographies are more than factual chronicles. Each book emphasizes the contributions, accomplishments, or deeds that have brought fame or notoriety to the individual and shows how that person has influenced modern life. Authors portray their subjects in a realistic, unsentimental light. For example, Bill Gates—the cofounder and chief executive officer of the software giant Microsoft—has been instrumental in making personal computers the most vital tool of the modern age. Few dispute his business savvy, his perseverance, or his technical expertise, yet critics say he is ruthless in his dealings with competitors and driven more by his desire to maintain Microsoft's dominance in the computer industry than by an interest in furthering technology.

In these books, young readers will encounter inspiring stories about real people who achieved success despite enormous obstacles. Oprah Winfrey—the most powerful, most watched, and wealthiest woman on television today—spent the first six years of her life in the care of her grandparents while her unwed mother sought work and a better life elsewhere. Her adolescence was colored by promiscuity, pregnancy at age fourteen, rape, and sexual abuse.

Each author documents and supports his or her work with an array of primary and secondary source quotations taken from diaries, letters, speeches, and interviews. All quotes are footnoted to show readers exactly how and where biographers derive their information and provide guidance for further research. The quotations enliven the text by giving readers eyewitness views of the life and accomplishments of each person covered in the People in the News series.

In addition, each book in the series includes photographs, annotated bibliographies, timelines, and comprehensive indexes. For both the casual reader and the student researcher, the People in the News series offers insight into the lives of today's newsmakers—people who shape the way we live, work, and play in the modern age.

Introduction

Funny Is Funny

FEW PEOPLE ARE neutral when it comes to having an opinion about Adam Sandler. The adoration his fans have for him has become legendary. On the opposite side of the argument, there are people who find everything about him distasteful and wonder what all the fuss is about. The argument rages on as his immense popularity grows. Since his popularity shows no sign of stopping, the argument will no doubt continue unabated for some time.

The argument exists because Adam Sandler has become one of the biggest box-office stars in America. He has achieved this rare position by being true to a strong personal ethic: he does only projects he thinks are funny and not those that others might think are funny. It is a disarmingly simple commandment that is the basis of practically everything he does.

Sandler's idea of what is funny has often resulted in the criticism that he not only lacks talent but that he is also partially responsible for the "dumbing down" of American culture. His critics feel very strongly about both of these points. Sandler has commented just as strongly that he is proud of his work and is not embarrassed by what he does for a living. He considers the ability to make people laugh a noble calling.

The comedy persona he has developed to accomplish this is not an original one. The idea of a shy, immature loser who is seemingly trapped in a state of arrested development has been a successful formula for previous comedy performers, such as Jerry Lewis. He has certainly added his own touches to that formula, such as the bursts of violence his characters are prone to or the boyish giggles he exhibits at the slightest hint of a bodily function.

Adam Sandler (left) is famous for playing the role of the hopelessly immature, but lovable loser, a persona made famous by veteran comedian Jerry Lewis (right).

It is this formula, as well as Sandler's contribution to it, that critics dislike and audiences cheer. Unlike some of his predecessors, Sandler has learned to grow within that formula as a comedian, writer, actor, producer, and musical performer with a likeability that has taken him to the highest level of success.

In order to succeed at doing what he thinks is funny, Sandler has gathered around him a close-knit group of coworkers, some of whom first met Sandler in college. He and his colleagues work extremely hard at their jobs because of the sheer passion they feel for the given project. All share a sensibility similar to Sandler's when it comes to what they think is funny. The finished product–whether a movie, a CD, or a website–is not accomplished by calculating what will click with an audience. Adam Sandler adheres to the simple rule that if he and his friends think something is funny, then so too will their audience.

Chapter 1

Stan and Judy's Kid

PROFESSIONAL COMEDIANS HAVE various reasons for choosing a life of trying to make people laugh. For many comedians, being funny is a defense against a cruel or unfeeling world. For Adam Sandler, his passion for making people laugh was discovered in the nurturing environment he found through his family, friends, and teachers. In one way or another, they all encouraged and supported his natural ability to make people laugh.

Family Support System

Adam Richard Sandler was born in Brooklyn, New York, on September 9, 1966. He is the youngest child of Stan and Judy Sandler, following older son, Scott, and daughters, Elizabeth and Valerie. For little Adam, the Sandler home was a place of love and much laughter. "In my house when I was growing up," Adam once said, "I was comfortable trying to be funny."[1]

That comfort level was aided greatly by his father, Stan, who supported his family as an electrical engineer. To young Adam, his father was a near-perfect role model. "He was twenty when he started having a family and he was always the coolest dad," Adam said proudly. "He did everything for his kids, and he never made us feel like he was pressured. I know that it must be a great feeling to be a guy like that."[2]

Adam's father was not only a great role model; he was one of the greatest influences on his son's sense of humor, both as a victim and a supporter. Adam discovered he could make everyone in his family laugh by doing a dead-on impression of his father's elaborate sneeze. Adam also discovered the classic comedy mayhem of Jerry Lewis, Mel Brooks, Abbott and Costello, and the Marx Brothers through his father. It was not unusual for Stan Sandler to wake up his willing five-year-old son to watch a classic Marx Brothers' movie on TV at 1:00 A.M.

Adam's mother also recognized his ability to be funny when he was very young and was not the least surprised by his later success. "He's always been funny," Judy Sandler said of her youngest child. "He always woke up in a good mood. We knew he would be an entertainer. The only one who minded was Grandma Anna. She'd ask him, 'Why can't you be a funny doctor?'"[3]

New Hampshire

In the summer of 1972, Adam's father accepted a job offer requiring the entire family to be uprooted from Brooklyn to the less hectic realm of Manchester, New Hampshire. The older Sandler children

Stan Sandler greatly influenced his son's sense of humor by introducing him to the work of classic comedians such as the Marx Brothers.

were more set in their ways and had a hard time adjusting to the change. For young Adam, the main concern consisted of making sure that there were G.I. Joe action figures to play with in Manchester. Once he was assured that they indeed existed in the New England state, Adam seemed fine with the idea of moving.

After the Sandlers moved to Manchester, Adam encountered a small setback in adjusting to his new surroundings. It occurred on his first day at Webster Elementary. During recess, while the other kids ran outside to play, Adam quietly gathered his things, left the playground, and walked back up the hill to his house. His mother, surprised to see him home so early, at first attributed it to a misunderstanding. She assumed Adam thought that like kindergarten in Brooklyn, first grade was only a half day. She brought Adam back after lunch as he tightly clutched his mother's hand.

New Hampshire: Live Free or Die!

Although born in New York, Adam Sandler grew up in New Hampshire. Nicknamed the "Granite State," New Hampshire's official motto, "Live Free or Die," can be seen on the license plate of every car in the state. Unofficially, the phrase teenagers use for something that is well liked is "wicked cool," as Adam did in the film *Mr. Deeds.* The Sandlers settled in Manchester, the state's largest city. Manchester is located in south central New Hampshire along the Merrimack River, twenty miles from the Massachusetts border and fifty-eight miles from Boston. According to its website, Manchester's nickname is the "Queen City." Like most of New Hampshire, Manchester enjoys the four seasons, with an average daily January temperature of 14.8 degrees Fahrenheit and an average daily July temperature of 70 degrees Fahrenheit.

Manchester was incorporated in 1846 and quickly became the world's largest producer of textiles. In 1998, *Money* magazine named it the "Number One Small City in the East." Its population as of the 2000 census is 107,006. The ethnicity of Manchester is mostly Caucasian, which constitutes over 90 percent of the population. Attractions in the town include the Currier Museum of Art and the Zimmerman House, the only house in New England designed by famous architect Frank Lloyd Wright that is open to the public. Manchester's Verizon Wireless Arena is the ten-thousand-seat home of the American Hockey League's Manchester Monarchs professional hockey team. Aside from Adam Sandler, another of the city's most famous natives are the members of the rock group Aerosmith, Adam Sandler's favorite band.

His mother thought the problem was solved except that Adam came home again the next day for lunch, and every day after that. Judy Sandler soon realized that Adam knew he was expected to be at school a full day but that he was obviously homesick and just could not bear going the whole school day without seeing his mom. He would sit at the table while his mother would talk to him, make him a peanut butter and jelly sandwich, and then walk him back to school after he ate. This continued for the rest of the week until Adam felt more comfortable with his surroundings. He eventually stayed in school during and after lunch.

Music and Mayhem

While his father encouraged his sense of humor, his mother helped establish his lifelong interest in music. She loved to hear him sing and actually arranged for him to perform at a local nursing home when he was seven. To the delight of the patients, Adam sang the popular song "Candy Man." At home, he would sing "Maria" from the musical *West Side Story* whenever his mother requested it. To this day, Adam shyly admits that he serenades his mother with the same song over the phone to get her to sleep.

Adam's main interest was still making his family happy with little jokes and impressions, such as mimicking Rodney Dangerfield, his father's favorite comedian. Adam would memorize the comedian's routine and constantly repeat it to his father's unending delight. "My favorite comic, when I was getting into it, was Rodney [Dangerfield]. . . . I'd walk around my house doing Rodney jokes for my dad, and he would laugh."[4]

When it came to appreciating what was funny, Adam was also greatly influenced by his older brother, Scott. Together they listened to Cheech and Chong comedy albums or watched Scott's favorite movie, Mel Brooks's *Young Frankenstein* (1974), until they memorized the dialogue. The 1980 golf comedy *Caddyshack* was Adam's favorite, and the Sandler brothers boasted of having seen it more than three hundred times. It starred their father's favorite, Rodney Dangerfield. Scott and Adam, with the help of their parents, learned to appreciate musical talent and comedy mayhem.

Fitting In

By his own admission, Adam was a decent student in his earliest years at school. His grades were good, and he was fairly popular among his peers. There was, however, one thing that got in the way of total acceptance by his fellow students. "I was always a little bit of an outcast," he once said about those early years. "Everywhere I went, I heard comments about being Jewish. And it would hurt."[5]

His father advised him to stand up for himself and fight if necessary. Not being much of a fighter, Adam resorted to the one thing that always worked for him at home: he made the other kids laugh. This strategy became one of the early seeds to help Adam become a class clown. His friends cultivated this behavior, and it continued to grow with their encouragement. By making fun of anything and everything, his reputation as a clown grew stronger. Adam proudly claimed that he once made an entire movie theater audience burst out laughing by shouting well-placed wisecracks and sound effects at the screen. Another of his more popular gags was popping out his dental retainer to the delight of his chuckling male friends and the disgust of his female friends.

A New Attitude

The seeds he had planted early on to gain acceptance blossomed into full flower by the time he entered junior high school. He now dedicated more time to being funny and less time to his schoolwork. His grades may have suffered as he got older, but his reputation as a cutup grew immensely. "Until sixth grade, I did really well in school," recalled Adam. "All of a sudden I said, 'What the hell. I can't take it anymore. I can't read and be so serious in class anymore.' I don't know why, but I just started goofing off. Instead of being book smart, I decided to have fun."[6]

This new attitude resulted in Adam's behavior becoming even more brazen than before. He proudly took any dares from his classmates to their rousing approval. Authority figures often had to tell him to straighten up or there would be serious repercussions throughout his life. Adam would heed the warning for the moment but quickly forget it when the next opportunity to do something outrageous appeared.

His new attitude of just having fun spilled over into his home life as well. When his mother became frustrated with his attitude, she attempted to give Adam the same kind of speech his teachers were giving him. Adam responded with his own brand of ingenuity. As he recalled, "One time, my mother was yelling, 'Why don't you ever try?' I had a tape recorder in my hand. When she stopped shouting, I played it back to her. She laughed for a half an hour. That was my life: doing something wrong, getting yelled at, and making the person laugh. Then it would be all right."[7]

Rock Dreams

Adam Sandler's formative years were not totally consumed by goofing off and hanging out with his friends. He still had a keen

Sandler grew up with a passionate love for music and as an adolescent he dreamed of being a rock star.

interest in music. When he was twelve, he sang the popular song "You're Sixteen" at his sister's wedding to rousing applause. He then pushed his luck by going for an encore with the Beatles classic "Yesterday," which got him booed off the stage.

He also performed the song "House of the Rising Sun" in a seventh-grade talent show. On the drive home from the show, his mother told him his voice had cracked too much while he sang. Thinking he had done a decent job, Adam took the criticism in stride and realized the pubescent condition was temporary.

By high school he was playing guitar in several bands with names like Spectrum, Storm, and Final Warning. He and his friends played cover versions of popular and standard rock songs that they practiced endlessly in Adam's basement. Adam and his friends actually thought a record producer would drive by, hear them playing, and then offer them a recording contract. The fact that this never came to pass did not deter Adam's love of music, which continues to this day.

Manchester Central High School

When he entered Manchester Central High School in 1980, Adam's reputation as a class clown had helped gather around him a coterie of friends also regarded as goof-offs and cutups. Their antics were not unlike those of the characters he would later play in his films. Asked what he was like in high school, his teacher Isabel Pellerin told *People Weekly* magazine, "You've seen his movies? That's the way he was here. I can't believe he's making all that money for doing things he was punished for here. I thought he would grow up. Instead, he grew rich."[8]

Adam did show interest in other endeavors such as sports and also served on the student council for a brief period. His most consistent activity was the drama club, which he belonged to throughout all four years at Manchester Central High. The experience of being in several school plays would contribute greatly to his plans after high school.

Aside from his interest in drama, the Adam Sandler of Manchester Central High School was consistent with the Adam Sandler he was in junior high, but with greater emphasis on mischief. He still found himself getting into minor trouble that often required the

Sandler sits in a classroom in a scene from Billy Madison. *In high school, Sandler was the class clown, indulging in the comic behavior that would make him famous.*

proper punishment. The teachers who reprimanded him often did so while trying to hide a smile. "Teachers would ask him to leave the class," recalled his high school principal, Bob Schiavone. "But they were laughing while they asked. He was hilarious."[9]

On some occasions, his misconduct resulted in stricter punishment than merely being asked to leave the class. The infractions sometimes required teachers to give him after school detention. He surprised everyone by being the only student to show up with a pillow and a portable television set.

Senior Year and Girls

By the time Adam reached his senior year, his reputation as a cutup was so entrenched, it even affected his relationships with

A Lesson in Love

In 1998, *E! Entertainment* reporter Jeanne Wolf asked Adam what was the toughest moment he ever faced in a relationship. He gave the question serious thought and responded with a poignant story from his youth:

> I remember one time a girl broke up with me in sixth grade on the phone when I was eating dinner with my family. My mom said, "Adam, Kim's on the phone." And I said to my dad, "See that? The girls are calling." I got on the phone and said hello. And then I hear, "This is Kim." And she tells me the girl I was dating wants to break up with me. I said, "Okay." I walked back to the table, and my Dad says, "How'd that go?" I said, "Good." He said, "What'd she say?" I told him, "She said she was excited to see me tomorrow." He said, "All right. Good job." And then I stared at my plate and tried not to cry the whole dinner.

the opposite sex. He had dated before then, but by the time he was ready to graduate, he had his heart set on Linda St. Martin, the prettiest girl in his senior year history class. Adam asked her out in front of his fellow students, only to be told he did not stand a chance. "This became a daily routine," remembers Adam's history teacher, Michael Clemons. "Now I think of Adam's success and wonder if Linda regrets it."[10]

Linda was not the only girl who became the object of Adam's affection. There were other girls in school who thought he was cute or funny. He was also ignored by just as many who, like Linda St. Martin, found him annoying and immature. No matter what the outcome though, Adam seemed to take both acceptance and rejection in stride. He never seemed to hold a grudge no matter how severe the transgression, a trait he would rely on greatly as an adult. His natural likeability and playfulness, which he would also rely on as he got older, kept him popular throughout high school with both sexes.

More than Just Funny

In spite of his penchant for fooling around, Adam did well in school. His natural intelligence and curiosity kept his grades at a respectable level, but to this day, he still downplays his intelligence. Asked once if his parents wanted him to be a lawyer or a doctor, he responded, "Ah, no. They knew the brainpower wasn't there. My sister's a dentist, my brother's a lawyer, and my other sister's a smart girl. There I am, the youngest and the dumbest."[11]

Adam may enjoy being perceived as someone lacking in brainpower, but his achievements prove otherwise. He scored very well when he took his Scholastic Aptitude Test (SAT), and although he was not quite sure what he wanted to do with his life, he applied to several major colleges. His SAT score, coupled with the years he spent in the drama club, helped him become one of only three hundred students nationwide accepted into New York University's (NYU) prestigious theater program.

His NYU acceptance allowed him to end high school on a high note. His parents were impressed, but Adam was more proud of being voted his senior year's class clown. "Those were the best times," he later said about his years at Manchester Central High School. "I loved summer, and going to school and flirting with girls, and trying to learn a little bit. I miss falling in love every five seconds."[12]

One Special Summer

Adam spent the summer before he started at NYU in 1984 visiting his brother Scott, who was attending Boston University Law School. Early that summer, they spent an evening at a popular comedy club called Stitches. In the mid-1980s, stand-up comedy was experiencing a big surge in popularity, so much so that it was not uncommon for comedy clubs to have "open-mike nights" in which audience members were encouraged to take a chance performing their own comedy routine.

Aside from showing him a good time, Scott had another reason for bringing his brother to Stitches that night since it was indeed open-mike night. The seventeen-year-old Adam, with heart throbbing and palms sweating, was convinced by Scott to take the stage. "If he hadn't said to do it, I wouldn't have thought it was a normal thing to do," Adam later reasoned. "I would have said, 'Mom and Dad are going to get mad at me.' But because he told me to do it and I knew that my parents respected his brain . . . it must be okay."[13]

Adam wiped his palms on his pants and slowly took the stage. Not sure what to say as he stared out at the roomful of strangers,

Adam resorted to his old gag of popping out his retainer. The only response was from a drunken patron who shouted out that the retainer made him sick. On reflex, Adam retorted that the man's drunken condition made everyone in the room sick. Adam knew it was not the funniest response, but it was the way he said it that made the audience laugh. The laughter, as brief as it was, became a moment that changed Adam Sandler's life forever.

Discovering His Passion

In spite of his nervousness and lack of funny material, Adam had suddenly realized what he wanted to do for the rest of his life. The audience's reaction to Adam's put-down of the drunken patron was a life-altering revelation for him. From the comfort he found in making his family laugh, to the delight of goofing off with his friends and getting into trouble with teachers who privately snickered at his antics, Adam saw his first nervous night on a comedy stage as an affirmation of what all those things meant to him. Having been unsure of what path he wanted his life to take, he now realized that more than anything, he wanted to make people laugh. "It was the first time in my life where I said, 'All right, I think I can,'" he later said about his first time on stage. "I became kind of obsessed with getting good at comedy. Growing up I wasn't that great at anything."[14]

Until he started at NYU in September, Adam Sandler spent every second of every day obsessed with getting better at stand-up comedy. He decided to keep going back to the different comedy clubs in Boston that offered open-mike nights to improve his performance and his material. Adam was not very good in those early attempts, often stuttering or on the verge of tears while still onstage. In spite of this, audiences could not help but like the hapless young man with the shy smile who did not quite seem to know what he was doing.

His inexperience and stage fright were hard to overcome, and made it extremely difficult for him to even open his mouth sometimes. Although most of the times he went onstage he thought the experience was horrifying, what kept him going was the rare occasion when all the elements clicked and he was the naturally funny person his family and friends knew he was. The problem

Sandler studied theater at New York University, whose alumni include Robert De Niro and Steven Spielberg, seen here as guests at a recent graduation ceremony.

was figuring out how to sustain those successful moments more consistently.

Adam was again aided by the support of his brother. Scott suggested Adam go onstage with his guitar and sing something first to help him relax. The trick worked, and Adam slowly began to improve his performances. After singing a few songs, he made jokes about the local Burger King and his grandmother's hearing aid. Now his stage fright was dealt with, and his material was beginning to show signs of the Adam Sandler soon to be known to millions of fans. By the end of the summer, Adam's mind was preparing to enter NYU but his heart was permanently entrenched in stand-up comedy.

Chapter 2

They're All Gonna Laugh at You!

ADAM SANDLER'S NYU theater scholarship was considered an honor since it allowed him to take classes at the world-renowned Lee Strasberg Institute. The institute was named for the legendary acting teacher who had helped pioneer a method in which the actor had to draw from and then use the emotions from his own personal experiences when playing a role.

That was a complicated concept for someone like Adam Sandler. His natural shyness and playfulness were at odds with the acting class requirements of remembering and reliving sometimes-painful emotional moments. He would rather spend his time thinking of funny things than bringing up the feelings of a painful past experience. "We were all supposed to go onstage and dig out our emotions," he later said. "At that time, I couldn't even look another person in the eye. I'm thinking, once I dig out my emotions, where do they go?"[15]

Brittany Hall

When he was not grappling with the difficult class requirements, Sandler bonded with other students who proved to be of spirits similar to his own. They all either lived in Brittany Hall–NYU's dormitory located in Greenwich Village–or had the same classes. Even though his dorm roommate, Tim Herlihy, was a law student at NYU, he proved to be a kindred soul when it came to what Sandler thought was funny. Several other classmates in the theater department, such as Jack Giarraputo, Allen Covert, Frank Coraci, Judd Apatow, and Tom Lewis, were freshmen who bonded

Producer Jack Giarraputo was a classmate of Sandler's at NYU, and he encouraged Sandler's early attempts at stand-up comedy.

with Sandler. These friends became Sandler's support group, encouraging his early attempts at stand-up comedy. They spent much of their time making each other laugh at things that other people would consider juvenile and immature. Their antics ran the gamut from blasting the music of Led Zeppelin from speakers placed in their dorm room window to shouting insults at pedestrians walking below. Eventually, several complaints to the NYU administration brought their antics to an end.

Some of the people who found them particularly childish were members of NYU's female student body. This made dating difficult but not impossible. Frank Coraci said of those days, "None of us were lady-killers but we did all right going out with girls when they didn't think we were too much of idiots."[16]

When it came to his acting classes, Sandler still struggled with the concept of using his own experience in creating a character. Although he later voiced regret at not having taken the classes more seriously, at the time he felt the classes were a waste of time and had a hard time paying attention. His instructors felt he lacked focus and concentration. Several of his acting teachers wrote negative evaluations citing that his inattention gave them great doubts he would ever succeed as an actor.

Sandler never seemed to take the criticism personally and remained in good spirits even when teachers chastised him. Teacher and adviser Mel Gordon ruminated on the best way to approach the fledgling thespian on his inability to make the grade. He decided to take Sandler out for a beer and told him he should change his major. Years later, while dining in a Los Angeles restaurant, Gordon saw Sandler coming through the door. Hoping to avoid a confrontation with the now successful superstar, Gordon tried not to make eye contact. "Sure enough, from across the room, he sees me," recalled Gordon. "He looks me over and says, 'Mel Gordon, Mel Gordon, Mel Gordon. You're the only guy at NYU who ever took me out for a beer!' He forgot the whole thing." [17]

Finding a Voice

The reason Sandler could take such recriminations in stride was that he had an outlet for his energy other than school. Whenever he had the chance, Sandler spent his time performing comedy, first on campus, and then later at such popular stand-up comedy clubs as Comic Strip Live. Since he was not yet at the stage where he could earn a living at it, he went through several menial jobs to make money. He had the most luck playing his guitar and singing in the subway for tips. He would simply open his guitar case and sing Beatles songs. When he got to twenty or twenty-five dollars, he would pack up his case, buy food, and go write comedy.

When he wrote comedy, what helped immensely was the support and input of roommate Tim Herlihy. When Herlihy went home for the holidays, he came back with a full page of new jokes he had written for his roommate to perform. Sandler was very impressed and thought the jokes were even funnier than his own jokes were. The two college friends became permanent writing partners.

In those early years, Sandler spent a lot of time trying to be like other comedians. However, with the help of Herlihy and other friends spurring him on to improve his act, he began to develop his own personal style. Professional comedians call this style their "voice." The more he worked at it, with his friends supporting him, the more the real Adam Sandler began to emerge. "My friends were always around to say, 'Hey Sandler, you're funnier than that,' and that's what kept me going," he stated years later. "They were always telling me I was a funny guy, and it took at least four years working in the comedy clubs until I believed it."[18]

Cleaning Up His Act

Sandler's perseverance in improving himself onstage eventually saw very big results. Open-mike dates at Comic Strip Live turned into paid performances. It was an important step toward landing the coveted headliner spot at the club. Like the other comedians at the club, Sandler kept working his act onstage in hopes of someday being that headliner.

On one occasion, NYU classmate Lorenzo Quinn, son of legendary actor Anthony Quinn, saw Adam's act and decided to

The Working Life

Adam Sandler's experiences with regular jobs never seemed to work out very well. In a February 1999 interview for *Playboy* magazine titled "Checking In with Adam Sandler," Sandler told interviewer Kevin Cook what he considered to be the highlights of his non-show business employment:

> I lost a job in a drugstore for miscounting pills. Then I lied to get work as a waiter. I said I had restaurant experience but after a couple of days the manager says, "You don't know what you're doing." [He] demotes me to the kitchen. Now I'm working with Brazilian guys who speak only Portuguese. I kept trying to make them laugh. I took a hunk of filet mignon—before you slice it, the filet is a long piece of meat—[I] put it up to my mouth and did Groucho Marx: "That's the most ridiculous thing I ever heard." [The] manager walks in and sees me. "Adam, you're fired." My next job was singing in New York subways.

While still in college, Sandler performed regularly during amateur night at Manhattan's Comic Strip Live. He would later be paid for performances there.

introduce him to comedy veteran Bill Cosby. Sandler performed his act privately for Cosby, an act that was laced with the foul language that was prevalent in comedy at the time. The veteran comedian listened quietly, and when Sandler was finished, Cosby simply told him to clean up his act.

Sandler took the advice to heart, and it made a huge difference in his level of success. His toned-down act allowed him to be even more like the offstage Sandler his friends laughed at so much. The club's talent coordinator, Lucien Hold, noticed the improvement in Sandler's act and saw Sandler as a breath of fresh air among the raunchier comedians. Hold took notice of the fact that Sandler could get laughs onstage even when the jokes he did were not that funny. Sandler could endear himself to the audience not by what

Bill Cosby advised Sandler to eliminate foul language from his act. Impressed with Sandler's sanitized material, Cosby invited him to appear on The Cosby Show.

he said but by the way he said it. He was also comfortable enough onstage to improvise observations about his family, fast-food chains, TV, and the occasional current event. Hold said, "With Adam, it was never about the material. He was just so likeable."[19]

Professional Show Business

Lucien Hold was so impressed with Sandler's improved stage act, he brought Sandler to the attention of Richie Tienken, the club's co-owner. Tienken had been the manager of Eddie Murphy, one of the most popular comedians of the 1980s, and if he liked a comedian, it could make a big difference in that comedian's career. Tienken liked what he saw in Sandler's act and offered to become his manager. Sandler quickly took Tienken up on his offer. Now Sandler's career not only had direction, it had momentum.

Sandler never stopped working on making his act better, while Tienken did what he could for the young comedian. After performing one night, Sandler was introduced by Tienken to Barry Moss, head of the Hughes-Moss Casting Agency. Moss had seen Sandler's performance and liked his breezy way with the crowd. Moss offered to become Sandler's comanager along with Tienken. Like Hold and Tienken before him, Moss saw great things in the young comedian. "[He] never prepared his material ahead of time," Moss later said about Sandler's act. "He liked to go out there, feel out the audience, and then he'd wing it."[20]

Television

Moss gave Sandler's career its biggest boost yet. He arranged for Sandler to audition for the very popular TV sitcom *The Cosby Show.* The important people who attended the audition included Bill Cosby, and everyone clearly liked what they saw. Sandler first appeared on the show on December 3, 1987. Sandler played Smitty, who was friends with the character of Theo, Cosby's teenage son on the show. Sandler proved to be likeable enough to be written in as a recurring character for several episodes.

Aside from his *Cosby Show* appearances, Sandler was beginning to make other inroads. He landed a recurring role on MTV's first regular show other than music videos, called *Remote Control.*

It was a game show that made fun of television, and Sandler fit right in to the format. Also on the show were comedians Dennis Leary and Colin Quinn, both of whom had big careers ahead of them. The show went on tour and gave Sandler a chance to see what life on the road was like. "That was a great time . . . we did all these colleges," he later said. "We'd come on stage and the place was so excited . . . I just felt a little bit like what a rock 'n' roll guy would feel."[21]

Everything he did in comedy now seemed to lead to something else. His appearances on *Remote Control* got him booked on MTV's *Spring Break* and *Half Hour Comedy Hour.* His career, fueled by his ambition, now seemed to be going at full steam. "He was always ambitious and he was very impatient," former manager Barry Moss said. "He was in a hurry . . . and he was right."[22]

Margaret Ruden

Even though Sandler's life was consumed by his burgeoning comedy career, he still managed to find time to date. Those times were rare since he still struggled with college and grappled with overcoming a natural shyness toward the opposite sex. If he met someone he was interested in at all, it would have to be in conjunction with the comedy he was performing. His shyness prevented him from meeting more people when he was on campus, but in the clubs he was more apt to approach people, feeling more comfortable in that setting than in school.

Women offstage occasionally approached him, and after one of his performances in a New York comedy club, he struck up a conversation with a pretty, young cosmetics executive. Her name was Margaret Ruden, and she was one of the women who did not find him childish but childlike. They started dating casually and gradually became more serious.

The Los Angeles Comedy Scene

By the late 1980s, Sandler had established a growing personal relationship and a growing comedy career. He had become the comedian to keep an eye on in the New York comedy scene. So much so, Lucien Hold decided to give Sandler the coveted headliner spot at Comic Strip Live. His decision was based not only on Sandler's growing popularity, but also on the young comedian's professionalism. "When a joke doesn't work, a lot of comics blame the audience," Hold later said. "Adam never did that. It was always his fault. He's very self-effacing and that's a key to his success."[23]

His climb up the ladder of success at the New York comedy clubs left Sandler at a crossroads in his life. If he wanted greater opportunity, he knew Los Angeles had more comedy clubs, TV roles, and the chance to work in movies. He had to decide whether to stay on and struggle at NYU to get his degree or put school on hold to take a chance on furthering his comedy career by moving to Los Angeles. The choice was easy for Sandler. He temporarily left NYU and moved to California.

He moved into an apartment in Los Angeles with NYU classmates Jack Giarraputo and Judd Apatow in the summer of 1990. The three friends commiserated with other young comics plying their trade in the Los Angeles club scene. Up-and-comers such as Rob Schneider, Chris Rock, Jon Stewart, and David Spade either lived nearby or also worked the comedy clubs that Sandler haunted.

After moving to Los Angeles, Sandler (center) befriended other up-and-coming comics such as David Spade (far left) and Chris Rock (far right).

Their days and nights were filled with coming up with new ideas for themselves and each other as they lived, ate, drank, and slept for their stand-up comedy careers.

When he was in New York, the important club Sandler had to gain recognition in was Comic Strip Live. Having conquered that, he set his sights on the West Coast equivalent. That club was called The Improv, and owner Bud Friedman, who had helped launch the careers of many famous comedians, took notice when Sandler performed. Friedman recognized what Sandler had to offer. "His act was not what we would call A-1 material," he said of Sandler's stand-up performance. "It was more about his attitude, his little-boy quality, his vulnerability."[24]

It was just this quality of little-boy vulnerability that set Sandler apart from the rest of the comics at The Improv and other area clubs. Sandler's act still consisted of the same things he had done to make his friends and family laugh when growing up, but he

Going Overboard in Film Debut

In 1989, Adam Sandler starred in his first film as Shecky Moskowitz, a waiter on a cruise ship who dreamed of becoming the ship's resident stand-up comedian. Filmed almost entirely on a cruise ship from New Orleans, the title was changed to *Babes Ahoy* so the production could emphasize all the beauty contestants on board who were bound for the Miss Universe contest in Cancun, Mexico. The low-budget film also starred Billy Zane (*Titanic*), Billy Bob Thornton (Oscar winner for *Slingblade*), Burt Young (*Rocky*), Terry Moore, and comedy legend Milton Berle. It also featured Allen Covert, Peter Berg, and Steven Brill, all of whom would work again with Sandler. The movie also had subplots concerning terrorists, General Noriega of Panama (Young), and the mythical King Neptune (Zane).

The production seemed jinxed from the moment it started. After the ship had left New Orleans, the camera crew realized they had forgotten the proper equipment, forcing the director of photography to shoot the entire film with the wrong lenses. It was released with little fanfare as *The Unsinkable Shecky Moskowitz* and quickly faded into obscurity. Years later, it was released on DVD and video to capitalize on Sandler's fame with the title *Going Overboard* and the ad line, "*The Love Boat* was never like this." It did contain several moments of twenty-three-year-old Sandler performing some of his earliest stand-up material, but that alone was not enough to save a film most people considered a waste of time.

had now polished it to a highly professional level. He held firm to his belief that if he and his support group thought it was funny, then it was indeed funny. It was often difficult to hold on to this belief in the face of other comics who were achieving greater success with angrier or more-topical material. Sandler found his niche in comedy by going onstage with the confidence to do whatever popped into his head and believing the audience would laugh because he knew it was funny.

The Big Chance

Having first made a name for himself in New York and then in Los Angeles, Sandler became one of the most talked about comics on the club circuit of both coasts. He worked very hard to achieve both the self-confidence and the stage persona that would allow him to do anything onstage and still get the audience to like him. His act would not be funny if it were performed by anybody else. His comic voice had become as individual as a fingerprint.

His managers, working hard to get that voice heard in the best possible venues, knew there was no better place for a young comic to be seen than on the long-running and popular TV show *Saturday Night Live* (*SNL*). The show was legendary for bringing national attention to talented young comedians. Sandler's hard work and his management team's persistence paid off. It resulted in his being brought to the attention of scouts on the lookout for new talent for the show's 1990–1991 season. An audition was finally arranged for Sandler to perform his act for the show's talent scouts and cocreator/executive producer, Lorne Michaels.

Different comedians have different styles, and those styles sometimes require different forms of preparation. Such is the case with Adam Sandler and his friend Chris Rock, who coincidentally was scheduled to audition for *SNL* on the same day as Sandler. Rock's style of comedy was not as freestyle as Sandler's, which allowed Rock to practice his prepared material until every word and nuance was perfected for the upcoming audition. Except for some silly songs and basic ideas to touch upon, Sandler genuinely believed his own strength was in being able to say and do whatever came into his head while onstage. If he froze in fear or

The cast of Saturday Night Live *poses in 1993. Sandler (top right) was originally hired as a staff writer for the show in 1990.*

became distracted by the pressure of the audition, the result could be devastating and keep him from being as funny as he knew he was capable of being onstage.

Sandler's agent Barry Moss knew better than anyone how important it was for his client to perform well at the audition. He made Sandler sit down, write out an outline of what material he would do, and then practice it over and over until the day he had to perform it. Even with the practice, the question still remained as to whether or not Michaels would be interested in Sandler's style of comedy.

Sandler and Rock were both flown to Chicago for the show's audition, which would include local Chicago comics. They were put up into hotel rooms for the night, and the next day they would perform their act in a club with Lorne Michaels in attendance. The night before the audition, Sandler heeded his agent's advice and practiced his act like never before. He also gave himself a necessary pep talk throughout the night. "I remember looking in the mirror," he later said, "thinking 'come on man, you better not choke.'"[25]

Even though Sandler had only been performing stand-up comedy for a relatively short time, he had progressed very quickly to a professional level. He had learned how to deal with his nervousness, maintain his confidence while performing, and he could endear himself to an audience no matter how outrageous the comedy concept. When his name was announced that late-summer night in 1990, he took a deep breath, squared his shoulders, and walked out onstage into the spotlight.

Original Thought

Sandler performed his usual act. It was the act he had been honing in his parents' house growing up, on the playgrounds of Manchester with his friends, in class when his teachers scolded him but secretly laughed, and in the clubs and streets of New York with his college and comedy club support group. According to Barry Moss, "He was incredible. It might have been the best stand-up that Adam's ever done."[26]

Being at his best may not necessarily have been enough for Sandler to impress Lorne Michaels. He had to wait before he received word on how he did at the audition. The news finally came several days later that he and Rock were both hired for the show's 1990–1991 season. However, Rock and several others were to join the cast as performers, and Sandler was hired as a staff writer. To his parents' relief, Adam Sandler took the short time allotted before starting the show to return to NYU to obtain his degree. Once he secured that, he prepared to join one of the most famous writing staffs in all of comedy.

The question still remained why Sandler, whose act was not typical *SNL* fodder, was hired in the first place. Years later, Rock asked Lorne Michaels what it was that made him hire the two young comics, since neither performer did impressions of famous celebrities or invented characters that could be used on the show. Michaels told him, "The reason I hired you guys was original thought. Anybody can do impressions."[27]

Those original thoughts were about to be unleashed on the widest audience twenty-four-year-old Adam Sandler had ever experienced.

Chapter 3

Live from New York

SATURDAY NIGHT LIVE first aired on the NBC network in 1975. Even though he was only nine years old when it started, like many fans Adam Sandler treated the cutting-edge sketch comedy show and its cast with the kind of adulation usually reserved for rock stars. Original cast members such as John Belushi, Dan Aykroyd, and Chevy Chase became role models to Sandler. The only hurdle to his appreciation was the 11:30 P.M. start time. He recalled:

> My big thing was trying to stay up to watch it. In the schoolyard the cooler kids were talking about [it] and I wanted to be part of that conversation. So I tried to stay up, and I'd make it to 11:00 and I was very excited; all I had to get through was the news. I'd usually get to about 11:20 and fall asleep. Then my brother would be carrying me to my room and while he was carrying me I'd be like, "Is it on? Is the show on?" He'd say "Yeah, yeah, don't worry, go to sleep, I'll tell you about it tomorrow." And so he would tell me what happened on Sunday mornings. . . . I loved Aykroyd. I loved Belushi . . . I loved Chevy. . . . The show was a major part of the life of every one of the kids I grew up with. . . . These are the funniest guys of our generation, so whatever they say is funny is funny.[28]

Learning the Ropes

Beginning in September of 1990, Adam Sandler was an official member of the groundbreaking series' writing staff. Sharing a small office with Chris Rock, David Spade, and Chris Farley, it proved to be not unlike his college days at Brittany Hall.

"It's Saturday Night!"

"Live from New York, it's Saturday night!" Those words were first spoken to open the irreverent comedy show in 1975 and have done so ever since. The original cast was called The Not Ready For Prime Time Players and consisted of Dan Aykroyd, John Belushi, Chevy Chase, Jane Curtin, Garrett Morris, Laraine Newman, and Gilda Radner. The cast, many of whom were also writers on the show, came from improvisational theater, such as Second City in Chicago and Toronto. They created dozens of memorable skits and characters that have become icons of popular culture. Lorne Michaels and the original cast all left in 1980. A few years later, Michaels returned with a new cast, which he has changed many times over the years.

Even though the cast has changed many times over the nearly three decades of the show, some things have remained constant to this day. Every ninety-minute show starts with what is called a cold opening, which is a sketch that has no introduction. The sketch ends with someone onstage shouting "Live from New York. . . . " After the opening credits, the celebrity guest host does a monologue, a commercial parody follows, and then several sketches are performed. A fake news segment called Weekend Update, in which current events are spoofed, follows a musical-guest performance. There are then a few more skits, and if time allows, the musical guest has an encore. At 12:58 A.M. eastern standard time, the cast, musical guest, and any cameo performers, join the host onstage to say good night. Lorne Michaels and his comedy alchemists manage to accomplish this twenty times a year with reruns in between to give everyone a short respite.

Members of the original Saturday Night Live *cast perform a skit with guest host Carrie Fisher (right) in 1978.*

The four young comedians spent an inordinate amount of time together brainstorming ideas and maintaining the grueling schedule required to put on a live ninety-minute show every week. Such conditions made it inevitable that they would all bond, with Sandler becoming especially close to Farley.

The week spent preparing for a live broadcast proved to be a high-pressured one for the young comic. Sandler got an apartment just blocks from his NBC office but spent little time there. On Tuesdays the entire twenty-four hours were spent coming up with and perfecting sketches that might be used on the extremely collaborative show. Wednesdays was the read-through, in which cast and writers exchanged ideas to be used or discarded depending mostly on Lorne Michaels's decision. Sketches would continue to be polished with a dress rehearsal on Friday night before a live audience. It was not unusual for Michaels to cut sketches either just before airtime or even in the middle of the live show on Saturday night.

If a sketch needed more people, the writers were often used for background and occasionally spoke dialogue. Writers who wanted airtime purposely wrote sketches that required more people to be in them. However, there were certain prerequisites to be met in order for a writer to get airtime. The show had evolved an unwritten code that stated a writer had to first earn the respect of the veteran cast and crew before he could be seen on the air or have dialogue in a sketch. This was accomplished by carefully studying the techniques of the other writers. It was also important to observe the cast members to see what they were particularly adept at performing.

Sandler spent most of his first year on the show learning from such veterans as Robert Smigel and head writer James Downey the process of creating the ensemble show. He learned not to take criticism personally and created funny material for friends Chris Rock and Chris Farley by observing what they excelled at most. He quickly approached the level of being chosen to be in background scenes that would give him the chance to get in front of the camera.

Airtime

Sandler got his chance on December 8, 1990. The guest host was actor Tom Hanks who had hosted several previous episodes. The moment America got its first glimpse of the new writer is crystallized in Sandler's memory:

> I remember actually my first skit. I was in a thing that Smigel wrote and that I helped write a little bit. And it was Tom Hanks and [cast member] Dana Carvey and I just came on, just had two lines, and I remember the countdown. I remember telling Hanks right before, "Hoo, I'm nervous." And he goes, "Hey it's going to be all right." I said, "Man, I feel like I'm going to faint or something." He goes, "Well don't."[29]

Sandler survived the 1990–1991 season on the show and made several more appearances. Lorne Michaels decided to give him the coveted credit of "featured player" the following season along with his writing duties. This was considered just short of being a full cast member. On most Saturday nights, however, he spent his time waiting backstage and pulling for the rest of the cast to succeed as the show aired live.

Lorne Michaels to the Rescue

The only way for Adam Sandler to get more airtime would be if veteran cast members left the show to pursue other projects. Although this happened every year, producer Lorne Michaels greatly resented it. He felt producing the show was hard enough without having to worry about which cast member would take their newfound fame elsewhere.

Michaels also had to contend with NBC executives who tried to tell him which cast members should be fired because they were not funny. Michaels especially resented this and found himself coming to the defense of Sandler, whom the executives found particularly unfunny.

Sandler was not aware of this at the time but did check in with Michaels whenever his confidence needed boosting. He ran ideas past the veteran comedy writer, sought his advice, and heard his voice in his head when he had to make decisions. When he discovered by the next season that Michaels had stuck up for him, Sandler saw to it that Michaels's faith in him was not misplaced.

New Characters

As Lorne Michaels had told the NBC executives, once viewers slowly got used to seeing Sandler, his original thoughts would be given a fair chance and the audience would like what they saw. The executives were wary of this philosophy, but viewers sided

Sandler performs on Saturday Night Live *as Opera Man, one of the many popular characters he created for the show.*

with Michaels. By his third season, Sandler began to perform songs and different characters, the likes of which had never been seen on the show. Almost all of them evolved from conversations with his friends and cast members.

Whenever Sandler got together with his friends, who now included several *SNL* cast members, they appeared to be spending their time just goofing around. Whether it was in Sandler's litter-strewn office or the late-night restaurants they haunted, they would often joke about each other or the people they encountered, much like jazz musicians playing at an after-hours club. The result was the creation of the characters and songs Sandler brought to *SNL*. These new characters were created not for fans of the show but for his friends. Trying them out on the air was a risk that paid off very well creatively.

One such character he created was Cajun Man. Dressed in overalls and straw hat, he responded to questions concerning his personal life or current events only with words that ended in "-tion." According to Sandler, "It started one night when my friends and I had gone to a restaurant and there was this Cajun guy in front of us who had a reserva'-tion.' Later, I started doing as many '-tions' as possible."[30]

Life at *SNL*

Adam Sandler still recalls his days at *SNL* with great fondness. When writers Tom Shales and James Andrew Miller interviewed him for their book *Live from New York,* Sandler spoke nostalgically about his experiences on the show and how it shaped his life:

> Backstage with Chris Rock, [Chris] Farley, [David] Spade was the best. Nothing was better than having a read-through. You stayed up all Tuesday night—all of us did that—and then we'd do the read-through and you wouldn't know what was getting on the show but you'd have an hour or so while those guys [Lorne Michaels and the other producers] were figuring it out. So we'd all go to China Regency up on Fifty-fifth and we'd eat and watch Farley eat more than us. Farley was so happy; I think we went there the most because they had a lazy susan. It's easier that way. That's all we did, we just talked about comedy—what we heard at the read-through, what was funny, what we didn't like, what we thought was going to get on, that kind of stuff. We lived for comedy. . . . We wake up thinking about jokes, we go to lunch together and that's all we talk about. I think we've become pretty obsessive with it.

National Fame

Sandler's characters quickly became pop culture icons. Sandler also did impressions of rock stars Bruce Springsteen, Axel Rose, and Eddie Vedder to popular acclaim. Across schoolyards and college campuses his catchphrases were heard incessantly. He also earned Emmy Award nominations for writing, along with the rest of the writing staff, for the first three seasons he was on the show.

With national recognition, Sandler's life took another turn. He was now being noticed and lauded on the streets for his characters and songs. Magazines and newspapers printed articles about him as the new star to watch. It was a new experience for the usually shy comedian and took getting used to. He still spent time with his close friends or girlfriend, Margaret Ruden, but between shows and during summer hiatus, Sandler began to seriously consider other outlets.

Raunchy Recording Star

Sandler's growing acclaim on *SNL* seemed to make him a natural choice for a comedy album. He recorded *They're All Gonna Laugh at You!* on a modest budget in New York and released it in September 1993. He coproduced the album with veteran producer Brooks Arthur. The album was a collaborative effort, with many *SNL* cast members and writers pitching in, along with girlfriend Margaret Ruden. The album was a huge hit and spent over one hundred weeks on *Billboard* magazine's best-selling list. Eventually it sold more than 3 million copies and received a Grammy Award nomination for Best Comedy Album.

The key difference from the humor his *SNL* fans were used to and what they heard on the album was the off-color language. The genial Sandler apparently still needed an outlet for the part of his childlike persona that would giggle at a four-letter word, and he found it in the recording studio.

His family, however, did not share the same feelings as his fans. "My two sisters and my parents don't even acknowledge [the album]," he said. "My brother and I slept in the same room growing up so it was the same humor me and him always did in the bedroom. But my sisters are nice girls and they were baffled by it. When my dad's alone he laughs . . . but in front of my mother, he's going, 'You stupid s***.'"[31]

Full-Fledged Cast Member

Sandler's album was released just in time to coincide with his fourth season of *SNL*. There were major changes to the cast that year, with several veteran members leaving the show and featured players now joining the ranks of the regular cast. One of them was Adam Sandler. Audience members now greeted his recurring characters with huge applause. He also got his old friend Tim Herlihy a successful tryout on the show as a staff writer.

As a cast member, Sandler performed songs from his album and also appeared in sketches in which he was often the central character. He was in several versions of "The Denise Show," playing the host of a cable show who cannot accept the fact that his ex-girlfriend Denise does not want to have anything to do with him. He was also Lucy the Gap Girl, a minimum-wage clothing store clerk along with David Spade, Rob Schneider, and Chris Farley.

Other characters soon followed. If an idea seemed promising, he jotted it down on a napkin or scrap of paper, as he had when he did stand-up. From these ideas came such characters as Opera Man, who read the news singing mock Italian while waving a handkerchief. He also played the overgrown Boy Scout named Canteen Boy.

An example of how he came up with some of his ideas can be seen in how he created a popular character he called the Herlihy Boy. "Most of the stuff I do on the show comes out of me just trying to make my friends laugh," he explained. "I was driving with some friends and I was in the backseat and I kept saying, 'Let me water your plants,' and they were laughing. So, I thought, I gotta do this on the show. And then I thought it would be funny if we kept cutting to [Chris] Farley yelling at me . . . that's my barometer. If my brother laughs, or if Judd [Apatow] and those goons laugh, I'm happy with it."[32]

Not all of Sandler's characterizations were popular. A creation he called Gil Graham never seemed to click with viewers. He played a bespectacled man with a strange way of speaking, who

Sandler appears in his underpants in a Saturday Night Live *skit. Sandler became a regular cast member in his fourth season with the show.*

commented on trying to get into different rock concerts only to be physically beaten for his efforts. Sandler eventually dropped the character, but the voice would show up again later in his career.

Clowns, Coneheads, Airheads, and Mixed Nuts

Like previous and current cast members of *SNL,* Sandler turned his attention to movies. In 1991, he had a small role as Dink, the sad, shy clown in *Shakes the Clown,* opposite Bob Goldthwait in the title role. Goldthwait also wrote and directed the strange comedy about the adult world of children's party clowns. It was not successful on release but has developed a cult following on video.

He had a small role in the 1993 film *The Coneheads,* based on characters created by *SNL*'s original cast. Many of *SNL*'s alumni and current cast appeared in the big-budget film produced by Lorne Michaels. Sandler appeared briefly as Carmine, an unsavory character who secures illegal immigration papers for the title characters. It too was not a success.

He appeared next in the 1994 comedy *Airheads,* as one of three not too bright heavy-metal musicians who inadvertently take the inhabitants of a popular radio station hostage. The film also failed to find an audience, but Sandler did establish strong relationships

In 1991 Sandler (right) made his movie debut as Dink in Shakes the Clown, a *film about children's party clowns.*

with producer Robert Simonds and costar Steve Buscemi, who played his brother in the film. Friends Chris Farley and Allen Covert were also in the cast as policemen.

The same year Sandler was in a film directed and cowritten by Nora Ephron called *Mixed Nuts*. The comedy concerned the strange characters involved in a Santa Monica psychiatric helpline. Sandler played a delivery boy named Louie who sang love songs on a ukulele. Ephron had written the character as a smaller role, but when she heard some of Sandler's original songs, she gave him more screen time. Steve Martin, a veteran of many early *SNL* appearances, headed the large ensemble cast. Sandler was in awe of the comedian and had to be put at ease by Martin during the film. "Steve would ask me a question," he later said, "and I would just look at his lips moving. Steve was like, 'It's okay, Adam. You can talk.'"[33]

Critics Inside and Out

Sandler, who appeared only in small roles, took the failure of all four films in stride as he began the 1994–1995 season of *SNL*. This season would prove more difficult than ever. The show itself had often been criticized when the writing seemed to falter, prompting critics to call it Saturday Night Dead. It had also been taken to task for being sexist in its humor and for leaving female writers and cast members out of the show. Such criticism drew fresh attention from NBC's executives, with producer Lorne Michaels again bearing the brunt of the blame.

The growing popularity of Adam Sandler and Chris Farley among younger fans of the show brought back the specter of such quips as Saturday Night Dead and other criticisms from the show's older fans. Much harder for Michaels to deal with was the fact that comments that the show was sexist and also biased in favor of Farley and Sandler were now coming from other cast members.

Janeane Garafalo joined the cast in September 1994 and left just six months later in conflict with producer Lorne Michaels. While she was still on the show, she publicly stated her dissatisfaction, calling the sketches juvenile and immature. Her comments were aimed specifically at Sandler and Farley and remain so to this day. "The only thing you could count on . . . when I was there," she said, "was if it was a Sandler or Farley sketch, it was on [the air]. That was the only thing you could bank on."[34]

NBC executives Don Ohlmeyer, Warren Littlefield, and others soon turned their attention to the faltering show. They had created a very successful hit for the network called *Friends* by personally crafting the cast of the show to make it work. Armed with this success, they approached Michaels about retooling *SNL*'s cast. Now that *SNL* had suffered a ratings slump and had lost many veteran cast members, Michaels could not defend himself as readily against the executives, who still felt Farley, and especially Sandler, were just not funny enough to stay on the show. He saw their reasons from a different perspective. "Adam has always been criticized by a generation of people who felt pretty confident that when the 'next big thing' happened, they would recognize it," said Michaels. "Comedy changes, and of course, part of it enrages the previous generation."[35]

Billy Madison

These behind-the-scene events were kept from Sandler. He continued the show's grueling schedule through the 1994–1995 season and even managed a few stand-up comedy dates. Tim Herlihy helped him write some new material for these dates as well as his *SNL* sketches.

Herlihy and Sandler had also been tinkering with a movie script they thought would be a good vehicle for Sandler's first starring role. They called it *Billy Madison,* a story about a rich but lazy young adult who must complete kindergarten through high school in six months to earn his inheritance. When they sought the opinion of Lorne Michaels, he thought the script had funny moments but overall it would not make a good starring role for Sandler. Sandler took the advice in stride and reworked the script with Herlihy on the basis of Michaels's comments and feedback from their other friends. They submitted it to several studios and were accepted by Universal.

The film encountered problems immediately. Sandler's original suggestion for director, who had once given Sandler a job in a TV commercial, was replaced two weeks into filming at the request of Universal executives. Tamra Davis took over as director

In his first starring role, Sandler plays Billy Madison, a young man forced to repeat his entire education in order to receive a substantial inheritance.

and tried to make sense of the existing footage while continuing the rest of the film. It was a daunting task, but the film eventually finished shooting and quickly went into editing for an early release.

Critical reaction to the film was harsh, but it opened to good business. However, Universal pulled the film from theaters after a relatively brief theatrical run. Letting it play in theaters longer would have made more money, but Universal did not explain its reasons for ending its theatrical run.

The video release of the film in 1996 found a new audience that made the film even more successful. "I'm always running into people who say, 'My kid's seen your video 18 times. He won't return it,'"[36] Sandler said.

Big Changes

Sandler had earned enough money from his films and other projects to make major changes in his life. His brother, Scott, now a successful lawyer, took over Sandler's business affairs. When his parents retired to Florida, Sandler bought them a home and a brand new Jaguar automobile. One of the biggest changes was in his personal relationship. He proposed to his longtime girlfriend, Margaret, in early 1995. He rarely commented on such things, but on this occasion he explained how he proposed: "I just popped it out. I feel loved to the point where I know she wants me to be happy, and I wanted to make sure she knew I loved her."[37]

The biggest change of all concerned *SNL*. Due to the pressure being put on him by his bosses, Lorne Michaels had no choice but to give in to their demands of firing certain staff and cast members. At the time, Sandler stated he had quit because the show had gone stale for him. Years later he spoke more openly:

> The guys at *SNL* protected me a lot. I didn't even know who Ohlmeyer was. I never met him. I just felt if Lorne likes me and if Downey likes me, I'm safe. Then I heard that at the end Lorne was having to fight for me to be on the show. . . . See, I don't know if I was fired. I don't know how it was handled. I just remember feeling like "Did I quit or did I get fired? I have no idea." All of a sudden, I just wasn't on the show anymore.[38]

His final appearance was on May 13, 1995. In the last sketch of that night's show, he and several other cast members who did not return for the next season, such as Chris Farley, were shown being eaten by a polar bear.

Sandler always maintained he had no regrets involving his time on the popular show. He simply took what he learned from the experience and put it toward launching a full-fledged movie career.

Chapter 4

Team Sandler

Adam Sandler did not let his dismissal from *Saturday Night Live* affect the momentum of his career. Instead, he plunged fully into the realm of film comedy, working hard to parlay the concepts that he and his friends thought were funny into what they all hoped would be successful movies. Dubbed Team Sandler, the close-knit group of creative collaborators helped mold Adam Sandler's on-screen persona. The ranks of Team Sandler include not only friends from school, but *SNL* alumni and cocreators from each successive project. Their lives and work intertwined to create projects with Sandler at the helm of starring vehicles that exploit his "lovable loser" persona.

Concentrating on his career as much as he did took a toll in other areas in his life. For Adam Sandler, it may have been the cause for the end of his relationship with longtime girlfriend Margaret Ruden. They announced their breakup through his publicist in September 1995. No reason was given, and Sandler has always been guarded about his personal life. He did hint at a possible reason for the breakup in an interview with good friend Ben Stiller while still in his last season of *SNL*. "Doing *Saturday Night Live* definitely affects my relationship with my girlfriend . . . because you feel so much pressure to do well that night. . . . That's why right now I'm working as hard as I can to make sure I get the best possible run I can get."[39]

Happy Gilmore

The hard work resulted in Team Sandler's first project after leaving *SNL*. It was a screenplay that Sandler wrote with Tim Herlihy concerning a young man who aspires to be a great hockey player

Game-show host Bob Barker punches Sandler in a scene from Happy Gilmore. *Barker agreed to appear in the film after learning that he wins the scene's fistfight.*

but his bad temper keeps him from being successful. Instead, he channels his energy into the game of golf and must learn to control his temper in order to win a tournament that offers enough money to save his grandmother's home from foreclosure.

The film is called *Happy Gilmore* and was inspired by a childhood friend of Sandler's named Kyle. Kyle currently plays for a

Norwegian hockey team, but when Sandler was a young teen, he and Kyle were invited to play golf with Stan Sandler. Kyle embarrassed Sandler's father by hitting the ball as if he were playing hockey and eventually won the game with his long, powerful drives. Sandler never forgot that afternoon, and coupled with the fact that *Caddyshack* was one of his favorite films, he came up with a way to put a new twist on a golf comedy.

Herlihy and Sandler knew that giving Happy Gilmore a vicious temper was a risky move since it might alienate him from the audience. Sandler explained his reasons: "Tim and I were looking for that edge to the character but we did a lot of thinking before we actually decided to give him a bad temper. We were aware that we were in danger of creating a character that people won't like. That's not exactly the kind of character you want in a comedy. But he's also a generous guy who's helping his grandmother, so I think people will think of him as a good guy. At least I hope they do."[40]

The cast and crew of *Happy Gilmore* were lined up but with a special addition included. Toward the end of the film, there is a scene in which Gilmore plays in a celebrity golf match with renowned game-show host Bob Barker. It culminates in a fistfight between the two, which Sandler thought was funny but would be hard-pressed to get Barker to agree to do. When the script was completed, Herlihy and Sandler sent the script to Barker. Once he saw that he ultimately wins that fight, he agreed to appear in the film. The film was then made on a small budget and again produced by Robert Simonds with direction by Dennis Dugan, who also had a small role in the film. Friends Allen Covert, Robert Smigel, Ben Stiller, and Kevin Nealon also appeared in the film.

The film was released in February 1996 to mostly negative reviews. Critics again described Sandler's comedy as juvenile and immature. Audiences did not seem to care and made the film a hit, especially among male viewers under twenty-five. Sandler tried to take the critical reaction in stride. He said, "I don't plan on getting good reviews. I don't think about that stuff. The only thing you don't want is for it to influence people's decision on going and judging for themselves."[41] The fans were on Sandler's side and gave his brawl with Barker the Best Fight Scene Award at the April 1996 MTV Movie Awards.

What the Hell Happened to Me?

Once he completed *Happy Gilmore,* Sandler and his team went right into the recording studio for his next album titled *What the Hell Happened to Me?* It was again a raunchy collection of songs and sketches created with his cohorts Frank Coraci, Jonathan Rosenberg, Judd Apatow, Allen Covert, Tim Herlihy, and Kevin Nealon. The CD had cuts with self-explanatory titles like "The Excited Southerner Orders a Meal," "Sex or Weightlifting," and the title song, in which he bemoans the loss of his childhood innocence.

The most popular song on the album was "The Chanukah Song," which was released as a single two months before the album's February 1996 release. Sandler had performed the song on *SNL,* but the response to the single took the recording industry by complete surprise. It became the most requested holiday song on Top 40 radio stations and continues to be a holiday staple every winter. There was more to its success than just the simple wordplay that listed other famous Jewish people who celebrated the Festival of Lights. Some of his fans could relate to the song's message about Adam Sandler's own childhood memories of the holiday season: "When you feel like the only kid in town without a Christmas tree, here's a list of people who are Jewish just like you and me."[42]

The album also proved to be very successful, earning Sandler his second Grammy nomination. He launched a popular twenty-one-city tour in the summer of 1996 to promote the album with his Goat Band. They were named for the goat Sandler voiced on the album that complained about his life. A performance with the band was taped in Chicago and aired as a popular HBO special. His core audience apparently could not get enough of Adam Sandler, who decided to try something different for his next project.

Not Quite *Bulletproof*

Initiated by Sandler, his next film was a departure from his previous fare. On his last season of *SNL,* Sandler had told guest host

Damon Wayans that he would like to work with Wayans on a project. Wayans, an actor-comedian who had briefly been in the cast of *SNL,* had found greater success in the cast of the similar TV show *In Living Color.* Sandler had found a property for the two of them in July 1995 that Wayans also liked, and production began the following year.

The film was called *Bulletproof* and told the story of an undercover drug agent and the annoying small-time drug dealer he is trying to bring into custody. Wayans played the agent, and Sandler was the dealer in the R-rated comedy-action film. It was only a moderate success when it was released in September 1996, in spite of the presence of its two popular young stars.

Damon Wayans and Sandler star in Bulletproof, *a movie about the misadventures of a drug agent and a drug dealer. The film enjoyed only modest box-office success.*

Part of the reason may have been in casting the stars in roles not normally associated with either actor. The film's R rating also may have contributed to its lackluster performance since it prevented many in Sandler's young audience from seeing the film. With only Robert Simonds producing and costar Allen Covert in the cast, it also had fewer contributors from Team Sandler involved than previous projects.

Whatever the reason, the film's failure did nothing to slow down Sandler's career momentum or the media's interest in him. He was gaining attention for everything from his dating habits to the way he dressed. Actress Alicia Silverstone was his companion for a time, and he was often seen with her as he wore his trademark baggy jeans, oversized flannel shirt, and baseball cap.

What's Your Name?

The habit of constantly wearing a favorite article of clothing was the most popular subject of his next project. He had performed his song "Red-Hooded Sweatshirt" on *SNL* in a duet with former Beatle Paul McCartney but did not get around to recording it until the 1997 album *What's Your Name?* The album was the first recording Team Sandler did consisting of all original songs without any comedy sketches in between. The foldout insert included the lyrics of the titles on one side and a board game involving Sandler's goat character on the other.

The fourteen songs on the album ranged from "The Lonesome Kicker" (about the tribulations of an NFL placekicker) to "Listenin' to the Radio," in which he lists the names of girls heard in popular songs, and also a reggae tune called "The Goat Song." The love song to his childhood sweatshirt was a popular single, but the album did not sell as well as his previous efforts. Fans were apparently more interested in hearing a mix of comedy and songs.

Undaunted, Sandler continued his demanding work pace. When he was not recording albums, writing and starring in movies, or performing live, he did date on occasion. Sandler remained true to the gentleman's code of not discussing the details of his personal relationships. The thirty-year-old did say in 1997, "I'm finally a person who could be in a good relationship. When I was young, I was pretty stupid."[43]

Making *The Wedding Singer*

Sandler was preparing to begin projects for 1998 when he received the shocking news about Chris Farley. Sandler always claimed his greatest joy came from laughing at and with Chris Farley. On

Sandler poses with Chris Farley in 1996 at the premiere of Happy Gilmore. *Sandler was deeply shocked at the news of Farley's death in 1997.*

December 18, 1997, that laughter came to an end when Chris Farley was found dead on the floor of his apartment. Sandler publicly stated that, with the exception of his grandparents, he had never experienced the death of a loved one and took Farley's passing particularly hard. "I'm still in shock," he said months later. "He was the man. He could make me laugh harder than anyone ever made me laugh in my life. I know that goes for anyone else who knew him. I loved him like a brother and I will always think of him. I know right now he's making Ben Franklin, Judy Garland and Jimmy Morrison laugh their asses off."[44]

After he attended Farley's funeral, Sandler returned to work on his then current film. It had the working title of *The Wedding Band* and came about the way many of his projects had in the past. Tim Herlihy said, "We wanted to do something set in the 80s and we were batting around ideas. People like to hear Adam sing and I just got married so it all came together."[45]

Before Herlihy completed the script, Sandler approached actress Drew Barrymore to costar as his leading lady, and she readily agreed. Retitled *The Wedding Singer,* the film became another full-fledged Team Sandler production, directed by Frank Coraci, produced by Robert Simonds and Brad Grey (Sandler's manager), and with roles for Allen Covert, Steve Buscemi, and Kevin Nealon.

The romantic comedy was different from other Sandler projects on several levels. Playing the title character of Robbie Hart, Sandler was not quite as goofy or juvenile as he was as Billy Madison or Happy Gilmore. Hart can be perceived as a bit of a loser since he becomes painfully aware of the limits of his occupation when he falls in love with a girl who is engaged to someone else. However, unlike his previous characters, Sandler shows Hart dealing with these obstacles like an adult and takes the audience along with him in his journey toward maturity. The comedy along this journey is derived from the fads, styles, and music that were popular in the 1980s, with less emphasis placed on the schoolboy humor for which Sandler was known.

One of the fads included the hairstyle Sandler sported in the film. The typical 1980s wig Sandler wore for the film proved extremely irritating. He half-jokingly said, "That was a wig that was

The Short Life of Chris Farley

Chris Farley was one of the most bombastic stars to ever appear on *Saturday Night Live.* He was born Christopher Crosby Farley, February 15, 1964, and grew up in Madison, Wisconsin. After studying theatre and communications at Marquette University, Farley graduated in 1986 with a degree in communications.

He was a member of Chicago's Second City improvisational group when Lorne Michaels cast him on *Saturday Night Live* in 1990. For the next five seasons, fans of *Saturday Night Live* either loved or hated seeing his huge frame and screaming voice thrust into the TV camera. Farley idolized John Belushi who, like Farley, was a regular at Second City in Chicago and then became a cast member on *Saturday Night Live.*

Like Adam Sandler, Farley was fired from *SNL* in 1995 but went on to act in feature films. After several small roles he starred in *Tommy Boy* (1995) with fellow *SNL* alumnus David Spade. The duo later made another movie called *Black Sheep* (1996). Farley then made *Beverly Hills Ninja* (1997), which brought him even greater fame.

Farley and Sandler often spoke about working together in a starring vehicle but it never came to pass. Try as he might, Farley's problem with obesity, as well as alcohol and drug dependency, was an ongoing battle he never seemed to control. He was found dead in his apartment from an overdose of cocaine on December 17, 1997. His brother Kevin discovered the body. He is interred at Resurrection Cemetery in Madison, Wisconsin. Like his idol, John Belushi, he died from a drug overdose at the age of thirty-three.

glued onto my head every day and put me in bad moods. I still have a little bit of glue on my forehead I'm trying to get rid of."[46]

Charming the Critics

When *The Wedding Singer* was released in February 1998, even some of his most ardent detractors had to admit this was a new and improved Adam Sandler. Critics, in their opinion of the film and Sandler's performance, most often used the word *charming* in their descriptions. The box-office return was better than his previous films, which meant more money for him since he was getting a percentage of the profit in addition to his $5-million salary. His fan base had now expanded beyond teenage boys to include young women as well. The film went on to win the 1998 MTV Movie Award for Best Kissing Scene.

Sandler sings in a scene from The Wedding Singer. *The film was released in 1998 to positive reviews.*

The reaction to the film proved to be a positive experience for Sandler in every respect except one. A tradition that had buoyed him before the release of every film no longer existed. Just before the film's premiere he said, "*The Wedding Singer* will be the first time I've done a movie and Farley won't be calling me up the night it opens."[47]

The film's success led to more magazines and newspapers requesting interviews with Sandler. He agreed to interviews in order to publicize the film but dodged questions about his personal life. He was, however, enthusiastic in talking about his work and his friends. When asked why he worked so much with the same people he said, "I like working with friends . . . because making a movie is a long process. . . . *The Wedding Singer* was a year and a half. I want to be around people I can have fun with. I don't want to be around new people. I feel safer with my friends."[48]

New Member and Project for Team Sandler

When it came to his work, Sandler was obviously more comfortable in the company of friends, but on occasion that circle of friends was broadened slightly to include someone on an even more personal level. Florida native Jackie Titone, an actress-model, was twenty-four when she met thirty-two-year-old Sandler. They met at a party where Sandler's eventual request for a date was politely denied due to her having to visit her grandmother for two weeks. This endeared her even more to Sandler, who began dating her regularly when she returned. The age difference meant little to Sandler, who joked, "When she was five years old and learning to read, I was thirteen years old and learning to read."[49]

Jackie Titone was now a member of Team Sandler as they began work on their next film. The idea for the script came about when Sandler and his friends were in the recording studio making his most recent album. In between takes, they would joke out loud about anything they came across. In this case it was an article in *Sports Illustrated* magazine concerning football team water boys. As the conversation progressed, the possibilities of turning it into something substantial crystallized.

Sandler and Herlihy immediately began working on the script. What they had in mind involved themes similar to their other films and *SNL* sketches but with a different twist. For example, with Happy Gilmore they created a character whose rage was apparent and needed little prompting. Unlike Happy Gilmore, this new character would be more amiable until pushed to a point where his rage surfaces. Sandler said, "Waterboy has a lot of rage inside and he finally explodes and tackles somebody. Then we thought it would be fun to do a movie about a guy, who instead of a quarterback or linebacker, the star of the movie is a guy who can tackle well. . . . I always enjoy writing with Herlihy about

The Members of Team Sandler

When it comes to helping their friends, few stars in Hollywood have proved to be as generous in spirit as Adam Sandler. His generosity is such that throughout his professional career, Sandler has gone to great pains to secure jobs in the industry for his close friends. However, his generosity can provide only the opportunity. It is up to his friends to have the talent that will sustain the job or career. Listed alphabetically, the following associates are just a few of the individuals who have proved themselves time and again when it came to being a Team Sandler player:

Judd Apatow met Sandler at NYU, and they lived together in Los Angeles. Besides being a chief source for Sandler to work out ideas with, Apatow has unofficially worked on the script for such films as *Happy Gilmore* and *The Wedding Singer*. Brooks Arthur produced or coproduced all of Sandler's albums and voiced characters in *Eight Crazy Nights*. Steve Brill appeared with Sandler in *Going Overboard*, several other Sandler films, and directed *Little Nicky*. Steve Buscemi first met Sandler when they played brothers in *Airheads* and has appeared in four other Sandler films. Teddy Castelucci, referred to as a "musician's musician," has been the driving force behind all of Sandler's musical endeavors whether in the studio or on film. He is also a key member of Sandler's live performances whenever he tours. Fellow comedian Blake Clark met Sandler while filming *Shakes the Clown* and has appeared in numerous Sandler films. Frank Coraci's association with Sandler began at NYU. He directed *The Wedding Singer* and *The Waterboy*. Allen Covert first encountered Sandler at NYU and later when Covert worked as a doorman at a popular Los Angeles comedy club. With the exception of *Punch-Drunk Love*, he has been in every Sandler film. He is also Sandler's opening act whenever he tours. Jack Giarraputo is also a friend since college and has produced or coproduced many of the films Sandler has starred in. Tim Herlihy has been Sandler's writing partner since NYU and gave up law school to become an *SNL* writer and producer. He accompanied Sandler into feature films as cowriter for practically everything Sandler has done. Tom Lewis met Sandler at NYU and has been the editor on most of Sandler's starring films. Rob Schneider was a neighbor of Sandler's in Los Angeles, appeared with him on *SNL*, and has had significant roles in several of Sandler's films, starring in four that Sandler produced. Robert Simonds began with Sandler by producing *Billy Madison* and has coproduced or executive produced almost all of Sandler's major films. Sandy Wernick became Sandler's manager after the comedian starred on *SNL* and left original manager Barry Moss. Wernick has advised and consulted Sandler on all of his business and creative decisions.

underdogs and guys who got abused, picked on, then fighting back. You excuse a guy's behavior or woman's behavior if they've been messed with a lot. They're allowed to do whatever you write. If you write that they yell at somebody, you're never mad at the guy for yelling. You understand where it's coming from. It's fun to write jokes for that guy."[50]

Making *The Waterboy*

Production began on *The Waterboy* in January 1998. Filming mostly in Florida (as a double for Louisiana), the production team had the clout to line up a stellar supporting cast. Aside from Team Sandler regulars, the film boasted Oscar winner Kathy Bates as

Sandler plays Bobby Boucher in The Waterboy. *The movie features several famous football personalities and established actors.*

Sandler's mother, TV's "Fonzie" (Henry Winkler) as his football coach, former NFL coach Jimmy Johnson, sportscaster Brent Musberger, and such notable football personalities as NFL Hall of Famers Dan Fouts, Lynn Swann, and Lawrence Taylor. The fact that such a cast was lined up was proof to Sandler of his success. He said, "That's how I know my life has changed. We write parts for people and they actually say yes."[51]

The title character, Bobby Boucher, is played by Sandler as a sort of cross between his *SNL* characters Cajun Man and Canteen Boy. He takes pride in his job as a team water boy but is taunted by the players to the point that he finally explodes and tackles one of them. The coach, who himself is teased unmercifully by a rival coach, talks Bobby into joining the team. The stipulation is that Bobby's overprotective mother cannot find out because she despises football. This premise progresses to the finale, in which everything depends on Bobby coming through during a crucial game.

Sandler enjoyed making the film, especially since his parents and girlfriend visited the set often. He got to show off his football prowess but did admit that some of the physical aspects of the film were taking their toll on him. He said, "We'd show up in the morning and we'd throw a football around. I threw my arm out. That's when I learned on this movie that I really am old. . . . After I threw the ball it was a lot of pain. I'm getting older."[52]

Just prior to the release of *The Waterboy,* Sandler received a rather dubious honor. He became the first former member of the cast of *SNL* to be the subject of parody in one of the show's sketches. It was in a sketch concerning the game show *Jeopardy* but with popular celebrities as contestants. Current cast member Jimmy Fallon played Sandler in a near-perfect exaggeration of his mannerisms. Since the show had always parodied current trends in pop culture, Sandler's growing popularity made him ripe for such a satire. After the release of *The Waterboy,* not even Adam Sandler could have predicted how much more famous he would become.

Chapter 5

Adam Sandler, Superstar

IN NOVEMBER 1998, *The Waterboy* was released in theaters across the country. Up until then, all of Adam Sandler's films had made money partly because they were produced on modest budgets. Even though each successive movie cost more than its predecessor, they consistently made money at the box office and even more so when released on video. In the industry, however, a film is not considered a certifiable blockbuster unless it earns $100 million at the box office. Sandler's movies had come close but had yet to reach that goal.

The Next Level

When *The Waterboy* opened it surprised everyone in the film industry, including those involved in the film. In its first weekend it made more than $39 million, a record-setting amount for a comedy at the time. As it continued its theatrical run, *The Waterboy* eventually brought in $161 million. Adam Sandler suddenly became more than just a consistent moneymaker with his films. The huge success of *The Waterboy* put him into the highest level of stardom, alongside such major stars as Mel Gibson and Tom Cruise. This overwhelming success solidified his persona as a goofy but lovable loser, to the delight of his fans and the dismay of his critics.

Reviewers who panned the film were not the only people who did not think much of *The Waterboy*. The studio that produced it severely underestimated Adam Sandler's box-office potential. Prior to its release, Disney Studios had presold the film to a basic cable television network for a relatively small amount of money.

They felt at the time they made the sale to TV that a major network would not be interested in paying a large sum of money for the rights to broadcast the movie. This decision potentially cost Disney millions of dollars when the film proved as popular as it did. Underestimating Adam Sandler became a costly mistake.

When the film's success made headlines, Sandler and his team of collaborators were already in the midst of several projects. He was busy filming his next movie and working out the details for the project after that. The success of *The Waterboy* apparently did not alter his focus. His producer Robert Simonds told the *Los Angeles Times* how Sandler reacted to the news: "It feels good but doesn't really change anything. We still have a lot of work to do on upcoming projects and it's important not to get ahead of ourselves."[53]

The quote came from Simonds because Sandler had decided to no longer give interviews to print media. This decision did not extend to TV talk shows, such as David Letterman's or Conan O'Brien's, since they aired practically live and very little editing was involved. He did not care for the way print journalists would be cordial toward him during interviews when he was publicizing a project but wrote scathing comments when the interviews were published. Often these same interviewers would review his films and likened the experience to everything from root canal to a lobotomy. "The press didn't really give him any respect," explained friend Chris Rock. "Everybody 'dissed' him and it's 'Now you want me to talk to you?' If I were him, I wouldn't talk either."[54]

Big Daddy

The project Sandler was working on when *The Waterboy* broke box-office records was called *Big Daddy*. It was a comedy about a single man in his twenties who adopts a young boy. It was his first starring role that was not initiated by him or anyone on his creative team.

The idea for the film had passed through many hands before it came to Sandler's attention. Columbia Studios president Amy Pascal thought of him for the role when she viewed an early cut

Henry Winkler (left) and Sandler watch the action from the sidelines in a scene from The Waterboy. *The film was a surprising box-office success.*

of *The Wedding Singer.* She held a meeting with him to discuss the project. She recalled, "Adam said, 'I'm not going to do it.' As he was walking out the door–and I was really devastated–he said, 'You know how we can make it work? We can make it work if we changed it so that I adopt the kid to get my girlfriend back.' Before, he just adopted the kid, but he wanted to do it with a twist, with an edge. And I said okay."[55]

Once it was agreed upon, Sandler and his team took over rewriting the script. Among other things, they changed the locale from Los Angeles to New York and also sought to make Sandler's screen character more mature this time than in previous films. There was still the usual quota of jokes based on body functions, but now that he was in his early thirties, Sandler wanted his character, Sonny Koufax, to project a more mature image than previous characters Sandler had played. He worked with the costume designer so that he appeared to be more of an approachable young man on screen and not the goofy loser of previous outings. Most surprisingly of all is that his character befriends a gay couple who is not the brunt of jokes but part of Sonny's inner circle.

The Sprouse Twins

Sandler knew an important key to the film's success would be his on-screen chemistry with the actors playing the adopted child. Because of child labor laws, identical twins had to be used to limit the amount of time either child would be working on the set. To

Sandler and the Sprouse twins attend the premiere of Big Daddy *in 1999. Identical twins were used during filming to limit the time either child worked on the set.*

ensure the proper chemistry, more than twenty-five sets of twins were interviewed. The interviews consisted of Sandler and each set of twins playing together on the floor with popular action figures. The chemistry worked best for Sandler with Dylan and Cole Sprouse, a set of six-year-olds.

When filming began, the Sprouse twins required the constant presence of their grandmother. Sandler encouraged her presence and even sought her approval. "I have some weird thing where I feel I need to be accepted," he said. "Their grandmother would come up and kiss me and that would make me feel better about myself. Then we could work."[56]

Other than Sandler and the Sprouse twins, many of his regular collaborators were involved in the film including Tim Herlihy, director Dennis Dugan, coproducer Jack Giarraputo, and costars Rob Schneider, Steve Buscemi, Allen Covert, and Jonathan Loughran. Several new additions were involved in the film including his nephew and niece Jared and Jillian Sandler and his girlfriend, Jackie Titone.

Poster Controversy

Big Daddy opened June 25, 1999, to the usual array of negative reviews but with some reviewers taking note of Sandler's efforts to mature his screen persona. In an editorial for the *Advocate*, openly gay comedy writer Bruce Vilanch praised the film's portrayal of a gay couple as a natural aspect of the story and not as the punch line to tasteless jokes.

In spite of these positives, the film elicited other negative comments. Some critics, noticing Sandler's attempts to make his persona more palatable to female viewers, accused him of merely tailoring his image to achieve a broader audience. Another criticism concerned many of the activities Sandler's character and his young charge indulge in for the sake of comedy. They run the gamut from public spitting to the larger issue of Sandler falsifying his identity to adopt the boy. If Sandler had done in real life what he perpetrates in the film, it would be considered a criminal offense.

The greatest criticism did not involve either the story or Sandler's performance. It centered on the poster used to advertise

Promotional posters for Big Daddy *featuring an image of Sandler and his costar urinating on the side of a building drew harsh criticism.*

the film. The poster depicted a scene from the movie in which Sandler and one of the Sprouse twins urinate together on the side of a building. Some critics felt that with Sandler's popularity among young viewers, it would encourage such unsanitary behavior. "I guess I understand," Sandler said about the controversy. "Some cities don't like it. But I got to let some cities in on a secret. I think people pee on streets even without my little poster."[57]

Greater Success and Criticism

In spite of the controversy, *Big Daddy* went on to make even more money than *The Waterboy*. It proved, among other things, that by doing what he thought was funny, Adam Sandler was one of the few show business personalities who was immensely successful at knowing exactly what worked best for him. This immense success brought a new round of criticism from social commentators who felt Sandler–along with such other popular film comics as Tom Green and Jim Carrey–were responsible for what many of them called the "dumbing down" of American culture. Because of the huge following the comics had among mostly younger fans, they were harshly criticized for their effect on American youth.

Sandler understood the criticism, but the amiable yet insecure comedian had a hard time not taking it personally. When he was still giving interviews to the press in 1996, his comments revealed the difficulty he had in grappling with such harsh scrutiny. He said: "I can live with critics who don't get it. There will always be some people who just don't get it. I just wish they wouldn't discourage other people from going to see my movies. . . . Maybe some day these same critics will look back at my work and think that maybe they were too hasty in their judgement. If not, I can live with that too."[58]

Adamsandler.com

As the harsh pronouncements increased, Sandler not only stopped giving interviews, he stopped reading his films' reviews. He immersed himself in his myriad projects, the first of which was his next album, titled *Stan and Judy's Kid.* All of the usual collaborators were involved, but unlike the previous album, Sandler returned to a mix of both comedy and song. Aside from such titles as "The Psychotic Legend of Uncle Donnie" and "Dee Wee–My Friend the Massive Idiot," the album included another installment of "The Chanukah Song."

Prior to the album's release on September 30, 1999, Sandler undertook a unique approach to promote it. One of the tracks on the album was called "The Peeper," in which Sandler voiced the mishaps that befall a voyeur. An animated video of "The Peeper" premiered on the Internet over 1999's Labor Day weekend. Created by animator Tom Winkler, it was the first of its kind made directly for the World Wide Web. The six-minute short premiered on the Warner Brothers Records website where it appeared for several weeks but thereafter would be viewed on Sandler's own website.

He announced the creation of "Adamsandler.com" in the same press release that announced "The Peeper" premiere. He explained the creation of the website was in appreciation of his computer-literate fans. He said, "There's a lot of pages on the Internet where [people] write about me, they make home pages for me. I wanted to do something strictly for the net and show these people I appreciate what they're doing."[59]

The idea proved to be highly effective. Because of this and other promotional strategies, such as an AOL online chat with Sandler that had more than five thousand fans logging on, the sales for the album were boosted dramatically over his last effort. It set a new record for the highest first week of sales for a comedy recording. The unique way in which fans could view "The Peeper" was a factor in the album's huge sales being accomplished without the benefit of a prerelease single or a traditional video. The website continues to this day, giving his fans a home base to view what their favorite movie star is doing, film clips, cartoons, and many images of Sandler's bulldog, Meatball.

Little Nicky

Riding high on the success of his most recent films and recording, Sandler started a new production company, which he called Happy Madison, to produce his next project. He had signed to star in the film for more than $12 million prior to the success of *The Waterboy* and *Big Daddy*. That amount was renegotiated by his agent when the receipts for those films made headlines. Just before it went into production, a new deal was struck. Sandler would now receive more than $20 million for the film and a larger percentage of the profit.

He was able to accomplish this because of the way he was now perceived in the industry. In early 1999, theater distributors named him the most popular comedy star of the year and presented him an award for the achievement. He opened his acceptance speech with a short yet succinct statement. He said, "My name is Adam Sandler. I'm not particularly smart. I'm not particularly talented. And yet, I am a multi-millionaire."[60]

Loved by Fans, Hated by Critics

Adam Sandler is not the first comedian to invoke the wrath of film critics for being considered juvenile and immature while a multitude of fans remains loyal. Silent-film comedian Harry Langdon is an early example of a performer who suffered the same predicament. Over time, the antics of such comics as the Three Stooges, Abbott and Costello, and the Ritz Brothers also suffered the same fate. In the 1950s and 1960s, comedian Jerry Lewis also garnered similar reaction to his films. In Lewis's case, the parallel is even more striking, since film critics not only did not like his films but also could not understand his fans' fascination with him. Here are several examples, from the book *Jerry Lewis Films* by Ted Okuda and James Neibaur, of critics reviewing the films of Jerry Lewis throughout his career. When reading the comments, it is not hard to imagine the same words being said today about Adam Sandler:

> His characterization grows monotonous, from this reviewer's point of view. . . . But audiences seem to adore it. We don't get it. That's all.

> To hail him as a major comic talent . . . one can only inquire, what has happened to the standards of humor, even those of Jerry Lewis fans?

> The gags are stale, the pacing is pure molasses, and the camera glues to Mr. Lewis' feeble prancing with royal fascination. He opens clattering doors, mashes unlighted cigarettes, drops the salt shaker in his soup—need we go on?

> Jerry Lewis, scraping the bottom of the barrel. Ten to one, only the most avid fans of this tireless comedian will find much diversion in this. . . . Open-minded customers perfectly willing to meet Mr. Lewis halfway may wonder if it really matters.

The renegotiated film that Sandler cowrote with Tim Herlihy was called *Little Nicky.* Sandler played the son of the devil, who must take over the family business from his unscrupulous brother. Outlandish special effects and countless guest appearances were a large part of the film's selling points. Aside from almost everyone who ever appeared in Sandler's previous outings and many new guest stars, the film included an appearance by his childhood idol, Rodney Dangerfield. As filming progressed in New York, Sandler was invited to appear on the *SNL 25th Anniversary TV Special* onstage with writers Tim Herlihy, Robert Smigel, and James Downey.

Back at work on *Little Nicky,* Sandler sported a strange haircut and spoke like his unsuccessful *SNL* character Gil Graham to play the film's title character. The humor in the film came from incorporating many of the same off-color gags he had performed on his albums, such as "The Peeper"; talking animals; and many scatological references. The executives at New Line, the studio coproducing the film, deemed all of these retreaded concepts acceptable. They also absorbed the cost of the expensive special effects and Sandler's salary, which combined to skyrocket the budget to $80 million.

New Line's parent company, Warner Brothers, had high hopes that *Little Nicky* would be a blockbuster hit. The film opened in

Sandler talks to a dog in Little Nicky. *Sandler received $20 million to star in the film and a large percentage of the box-office profits.*

November 2000 to less than spectacular business. When it returned less than $30 million at the box office, coupled with other unsuccessful aspects of the company, Warner's stock plummeted. Industry experts were again writing articles bemoaning Sandler's inane humor, but now asked if he was worth his multimillion-dollar salary.

Remaking a Classic

A good part of that multimillion-dollar salary went toward a major purchase. In April 2001, Sandler bought the house in Malibu he had been leasing for himself and Jackie Titone for the last six months. The three-thousand-square-foot, three-bedroom home cost him more than $3 million, with another half million to furnish it and add an expensive art collection. The home was built in 1947 on a bluff overlooking the Pacific Ocean and sported high glass walls for a scenic view and a deck to accommodate up to a hundred guests.

Adam Sandler helped pay off the large purchase with his next project. It was a remake of the beloved 1936 American film classic *Mr. Deeds Goes to Town* that had starred Gary Cooper and was directed by the legendary Frank Capra. It told the story of a small-town man who inherits a large sum of money and then must fight unscrupulous powers that look to take it away from him because he sought to help the underprivileged.

Due to the disappointing returns on *Little Nicky,* Sandler was offered $20 million for *Mr. Deeds* but with an important stipulation added to the salary. He would be paid that amount only if the film made more than $100 million at the box office.

Undertaking a remake of such a respected film did not endear Sandler to film enthusiasts who anticipated a mockery would be made of the revered film. Classic movie fans and critics may have felt that way because of Sandler's last film as well as early reports that were coming from one of the location sites. After three weeks of filming in New Milford, Connecticut, local newspapers claimed that the more than one hundred members of the cast and crew did not leave the small town in the pristine condition they had found it. Local resident Jim Kick said, "They came in and did just about

Winona Ryder and Sandler star in Mr. Deeds, *a remake of the 1936 film* Mr. Deeds Goes to Town *starring Gary Cooper.*

anything they wanted to do. They shut the street down for a week straight. There was nowhere to park and I lost business."[61]

Following the events in New Milford, filming in New York City encountered other problems. Sandler's costar in the film, Winona Ryder, took a tumble during one scene in which she and

Sandler rode bikes around Central Park. The actress said, "I was in heels and my heel caught in the pedal. The funniest thing is we were just standing there and I was showing off like an idiot. Suddenly, I was on the ground and he was like, 'Are you okay?' I got up and was like, 'Yeah, I'm fine. No problem . . . the next morning, oh god my arm hurt!"[62] It turned out that she had broken her arm.

Back on Top

When the finished product was in theaters the following year, most film critics wasted no time comparing it negatively to the original. However, now that Sandler had returned to a formula that included his usual array of PG-13 humor for his young male fans, and a sweet love story for his growing number of female fans, he was back on top at the box office.

Team Sandler had created a hit film with their concept of updating a classic for modern audiences who were not as familiar with the original as critics were. The finished product actually did not veer too much from the first version, aside from being updated for contemporary audiences. Sandler played Deeds as a

Common Threads

In watching Adam Sandler movies, certain common aspects begin to emerge in the majority of them. Recurring elements in Sandler films include the fact that almost all of his characters have names that end in Y or the Y-sound, such as Shecky, Louie, Billy, Happy, Archie, Robbie, Bobby, Sonny, Barry, Nicky, and Davey. In many films, the lead female character often has a V in her first and sometimes last name, such as Veronica Vaughn in *Billy Madison,* Virginia Venit in *Happy Gilmore,* Vicki Vallencourt in *The Waterboy,* and Valeri in *Little Nicky.* Often these characters are played by blonde actresses or actresses who dye their hair blonde.

Some common aspects are subtler than just name recognition. Since Sandler has acknowledged being a fan of professional wrestling, many of his films either reference wrestling, such as *Billy Madison* and *The Waterboy,* or have wrestling or wrestlers in them, like *Big Daddy, Mr. Deeds, Little Nicky,* and *Anger Management.* Also worth noting is that *Billy Madison, The Waterboy,* and *Mr. Deeds* are all characters who are cared for by older matrons.

pizzeria owner from a small town in New Hampshire, one not unlike Sandler's own childhood home of Manchester. The film was also updated to include references to tabloid journalists who exploit celebrities.

By the end of its original theatrical run, *Mr. Deeds* made more than $126 million at the box office. It earned Sandler his salary, but at the time the film was being readied for release, such concerns seemed of little consequence. The events of September 11, 2001, occupied the thoughts of Adam Sandler and the entire world.

Chapter 6

Changes

ADAM SANDLER SPENT most of 2001 completing *Mr. Deeds,* renovating his new home, and organizing his schedule for upcoming projects. Most of these projects entailed some subtle and some not so subtle changes in his perceived persona. Since he and his audience were both getting older, he recognized the importance of finding projects that would allow him to be accepted in roles beyond that of an immature man trapped in a state of arrested development. Sustaining a lengthy film career would require a mature persona to successfully emerge. Off-screen events, however, took precedence in Sandler's life.

September 11, 2001

In June, Sandler took time out of his busy schedule to pay his respects to the late Anthony Quinn. The eighty-six-year-old film legend had died June 3 of respiratory failure. The following Sunday, Sandler flew to Rhode Island for the actor's funeral, which was attended by many dignitaries and celebrities. As he often had within his circle of friends, Sandler remained close to Quinn's son Lorenzo and was there not as a celebrity, but as a supportive friend in a time of need.

Three months later to the day, Adam Sandler awoke to the startling news of September 11. The shock and horror of those events affected the entire world but nowhere more so than in the United States. The country dealt with its grief with an outpouring of humanitarian efforts and a rallying spirit of unity.

Many notable personalities felt they could rally the country and organize fund-raising efforts in which their celebrity could be used in a positive way. The two largest events were organized and put on in record time. The biggest names in show business were involved in these events, but only a small handful were involved in both of them. One of those few stars who were involved in both was Adam Sandler.

The first was called *America: A Tribute to Heroes.* Organized and aired just ten days after the attacks, it was a two-hour telethon appearing on all the major networks simultaneously to raise money for the victims of the September 11 attacks and their families. A roster of the biggest names in show business appeared on air to recount brave and poignant stories of the victims and heroes of the tragedy, while still others performed appropriate songs for the event. Sandler did neither, remaining in the background with other celebrities who manned the phone banks and took pledges through the night. He did join in on the finale consisting of all the participants singing "America the Beautiful." The record number of viewers contributed more than $150 million worldwide.

A month later, Sandler was one of the many luminaries who took part in *The Concert for New York City.* He volunteered to pay tribute to the men and women who worked so diligently in the rescue and cleanup effort of the World Trade Center. Taking place in Madison Square Garden with a capacity audience of police, fire, and emergency personnel in attendance for free, the massive concert was aired live on HBO. Sandler resurrected his Opera Man character for an appropriate performance that had the crowd on its feet. Police officer David Isaksen said, "The concert was a break from the horror, a little piece of heaven on earth after being in hell for six weeks. As a cop, you are always called on to do things for other people and that night, there were all these people doing something for us."[63]

Eight Crazy Nights

After his appearances at the September 11 events, Sandler was hard at work on his numerous projects. The next scheduled film was a departure for Team Sandler, an animated musical feature that took its title from a line in his popular "The Chanukah Song." Called *Eight Crazy Nights,* Sandler voiced several of the characters, in-

Sandler, Will Ferrell, and Mike Myers (left to right) appeared at a 2001 benefit for the personnel involved in rescue and cleanup after the September 11, 2001, terrorist attacks.

cluding the lead role of Davey Stone. Animation director Seth Kearsley used a picture of nineteen-year-old Sandler as a model for the character's appearance. Davey's many pranks land him in the custody of a little old man named Whitey Duvall and his twin sister Eleanor, both voiced by Sandler. Together, they try to teach the unruly Davey the true spirit of the holiday season.

The project had been announced in early 1999 but took quite some time to complete. The idea of being animated was intriguing to Sandler, and he found it quite jarring to see himself in cartoon form. "They made me better looking then I really am," he said. "When I'm shooting a real movie, I see the directors who are shooting me go,

Memories of Childhood Hanukkah

The idea of making *Eight Crazy Nights* was inspired by Sandler's own childhood memories of the holiday. In 2002, *Teen People* magazine interviewed him online and asked him about those memories:

> I loved Hanukkah when I was a kid. My parents would hide my presents in this one closet, and I'd wait for everyone to go to sleep and walk to the closet door. I remember saying, "I better not open the door because I might get caught." When I was eight, I opened the door and my mother hadn't wrapped the presents yet, and I saw what I got. I felt so bad because I had ruined the surprise. It was the only Hanukkah I couldn't enjoy.

'Oh my god, don't come any closer.' But in Animationville, they give you whatever you want to make you look pretty."[64]

The film was released in November 2002 to less than spectacular business. Its lackluster success was attributed to everything from the raunchy jokes–quite startling for a holiday-themed animation film–to the retread characters and situations from previous Sandler efforts. The character of little Whitey Duvall, among others, had been heard on the album *Stan and Judy's Kid* and was also in *Little Nicky.*

The Greatest Challenge

Continuing his breakneck pace, Sandler's next project was the first in which Team Sandler had no involvement at all. The result would be the most challenging work of his career. Paul Thomas Anderson, a young writer-director of several critically acclaimed films, was a big fan of Adam Sandler's work. Anderson devised the project based on something he read involving a civil engineering student named David Phillips. Phillips discovered a legal loophole in a promotional campaign to gain frequent-flyer miles through the purchase of inexpensive pudding cups. For an investment of only three thousand dollars, Phillips earned more than a million airline miles that he used to fly anywhere in the world at no charge. Anderson met with Phillips, bought the rights to his story, and used it to come up with *Punch-Drunk Love.*

The project was specifically written with Adam Sandler in mind for the lead role. He played Barry Egan, a small-time San Fernando

Valley manufacturer of novelty toilet plungers. Barry's life outside of his business is not a happy one. He is constantly harassed by his seven sisters, suffers from an extremely violent temper, and longs to have something more meaningful in his life. Looking to give his life a greater sense of purpose, he discovers the frequent-flyer program just as one of his sisters has set him up on a blind date. The young woman and Barry are apparently meant for each other, but in order for him to continue the relationship, Barry must confront the barriers in his life that render him socially handicapped. One such impediment is a small-time crook who has been blackmailing him and threatening him with violence. The complex plot and

Davey Stone (left) in Eight Crazy Nights, *a cartoon movie based on Sandler's childhood memories of the Jewish holiday Hanukkah, is modeled after Sandler at the age of nineteen.*

characters of the adult comedy-drama were presented in a very stylized manner that included animated color stripes between scenes and a very offbeat soundtrack.

Anderson instinctively knew that Sandler was capable of portraying the complex character. They worked together closely on the project, with Anderson coming away very impressed with Sandler's ability to tackle the demands of the role. "There's a real streak of mystery to him, a real dangerous quality," said Anderson. "And it's about keeping himself honest. . . . Adam Sandler doesn't do press interviews. There are not a lot of stars who have become so famous so quickly who have never used the media to present an image. You don't know who he is. He can be the character."[65]

Meeting the Challenge

Knowing that *Punch-Drunk Love* was not typical of Sandler's previous films, Anderson was mindful of presenting it the best way

Sandler plays Barry Egan in Punch-Drunk Love. *Egan's complex character proved the most challenging role of Sandler's career to date.*

possible. It first appeared at prestigious film festivals, such as the New York Film Festival and the Cannes Film Festival in France. The commercial success of the film hinged entirely on the reception it would receive at these festivals.

The reception for the film at each venue was overwhelming praise, with Anderson being named Best Director at the Cannes Film Festival. Sandler's powerful performance also received much praise and changed many people's opinion about his ability as an actor. After each screening, Sandler, Anderson, and others were present to answer questions from the audience, and the reluctant star found himself being asked if the challenging role was an intentional career move. "It's not like I sit at home thinking about how to challenge myself next," he said.[66]

The praise for the film continued unabated. After its run at various film festivals and colleges, *Punch-Drunk Love* was given a limited release in select theaters in New York, Los Angeles, and Toronto in the fall of 2002. It received even greater praise, with Sandler garnering the best reviews of his career. He was eventually nominated for a Golden Globe Award, and ads were seen in entertainment industry papers touting him for an Oscar nomination.

Although he was not nominated, the opinion was unanimously held that Adam Sandler was capable of much more than previously thought. Several critics even saw similarities between the dark aspects of Barry Egan and previous Sandler characters such as Happy Gilmore or Bobby Boucher in *The Waterboy*. The critics also took note of the fact that the more mature Adam Sandler was not only perceived as capable of growth within the persona he had created, but was now accepted as an actor of greater depth beyond the confines of that persona.

Making It Official

There were even more changes in store for Adam Sandler than his growing image as a respected actor. There had been much speculation in the press concerning his relationship with girlfriend Jackie Titone and when or if they would marry. A tabloid journalist even attempted to get an exclusive comment from Sandler's father by presenting him with a bouquet of flowers. Stan Sandler made no comment but took the flowers with a smile.

In June 2002, Sandler's publicist gave a statement to the press ending the speculation. Adam Sandler and Jackie Titone were officially engaged. In Sandler's own words, he described how difficult it was to no longer call Jackie Titone his girlfriend but his fiancée. He said she understood how difficult the transition was for him.

He went on to explain how the proposal came about. "I got her one of those rings you ladies like to wear," he said. "I don't know how smooth I was but she said 'yeah.' We went out and we hung out all night and at the end of the night, I managed to pull it off. She called her mom and her sister on her cell phone immediately and said, 'It's on, it's happening!'"[67]

Anger Management

Sandler proposed to his fiancée during a day off from filming *Anger Management* with costar Jack Nicholson. The casting of the established film veteran with the younger star was not easily accomplished. Revolution Studio, which was coproducing the film with Happy Madison, courted Nicholson for some time. Nicholson was sent the script back in 2001 and read it several times. The producers did not hear from him for more than a month and thought his interest had waned. Suddenly, Nicholson agreed to be in the film and the comedy began filming in early 2002.

It was one of the first movies to be partially filmed in post–September 11 New York. Nicholson and Sandler had both participated in the September 11 telethon, and since New York had been economically devastated by the terrorist attacks, both actors knew filming there would bring badly needed revenue to the city.

On the surface, *Anger Management* seemed very similar to other Adam Sandler films. He played Dave Buznik, a hapless low-level advertising executive who is inadvertently court ordered to take an anger management course taught by the strange yet popular Buddy Rydell, played by Nicholson. As the events unfold, however, it turns out that Sandler's character is not as much a victim of circumstance as he first appears. Rydell's unorthodox treatment

Jack Nicholson and Sandler star in Anger Management *in 2003. It was one of the highest-grossing films in which Nicholson has ever appeared.*

may be hard for Buznik to deal with, but it does lead him to confront many things in his life he has been repressing for too long.

Both stars got along very well during the making of the movie, and their chemistry was well received by audiences. When the film opened in theaters in April 2003, like *The Waterboy,* it again set new box-office records for an opening weekend of a comedy. It eventually made more than $133 million, one of the highest-grossing films Jack Nicholson has appeared in. For Adam Sandler, it was his fourth starring film to make more than $100 million. It was also the first film in which he played a fully mature and responsible young man. He was changing his image, and his fans liked the new Adam Sandler.

When the film opened, Sandler also took it upon himself to send copies to military bases overseas during the Iraq war. This version of the film was slightly different in that a five-minute prologue was added. It consisted of Sandler personally thanking the troops for what they were doing in the war against Saddam Hussein.

A Bachelor No More

With a solid career established as a major motion picture star, Adam Sandler's life was about to go through one of the biggest changes that any person could experience. On June 22, 2003, he and Jackie Titone were married in Malibu at the oceanfront estate of popular TV personality Dick Clark. Four hundred guests were invited to witness the Jewish ceremony in which Sandler wore a tuxedo and a white yarmulke, a traditional head covering for men during religious services.

The ceremony was not completely traditional, as touches of Sandler's trademark humor were apparent. The bride was preceded by Sandler's bulldog, Meatball, who also wore a yarmulke and tuxedo as he lumbered down the aisle with the wedding ring on his back. The bride gave the groom a mate for his dog, a female bulldog named Matzoball. Following the ceremony, Sandler serenaded his bride with a song he wrote for the event, very much like Robbie Hart in *The Wedding Singer.* Dylan Sprouse, costar of *Big Daddy,* commented about the song. "He sang her weight and how 'she'd rather not be with me except in a mall.' She was laughing and crying,"[68] said Sprouse.

Many of the guests in attendance were some of the biggest names in show business. They danced to the live band, enjoyed the wedding cake made of a cupcake tower, and played video arcade games that were set up at the estate for the reception. The party eventually ended around 2:00 A.M. with guests receiving a complimentary box of doughnuts. It contained a card with a picture of the newlyweds' bulldogs on it that read, "Eat your doughnuts before we do."[69]

Hard at Work

The ceremony was a short respite from Sandler's busy schedule. He was in the midst of filming his next movie titled *50 First Dates.*

The romantic comedy reunited him with *Wedding Singer* costar Drew Barrymore. Sandler plays Henry Roth, a veterinarian who falls in love with Barrymore's character, Lucy Whitmore. The comedy centers on the fact that Lucy suffers from short-term memory loss, requiring Henry to constantly romance her anew every single day.

The production was filmed mostly in Hawaii with many of Sandler's creative team involved in front of and behind the camera. Sandler again contributed to the screenplay along with longtime writing partner Tim Herlihy and at least four other writers receiving screen credit. Sandler liked the original story and the

Letter from Dad

When Adam Sandler and Jackie Titone married in June 2003, Sandler's website hosted pictures of the event. Another feature of the site is the periodic letters sent by Stan Sandler to his son. Like his critics, Stan Sandler often reprimands his son for his immaturity but also updates him on family happenings. This is the letter a few weeks after Adam Sandler's marriage.

> Adam,
> I didn't think I was going to have to write again. Everything was going so well. Your marriage to Jackie was terrific. Tyler's graduation was wonderful. Tori's being in the top five percent of her class is great. Jackie's sister getting into medical school is marvelous. Jillian going to middle school and Jared being a senior in elementary school is fantastic. Everyone is growing up. AT LEAST EVERYONE EXCEPT YOU AND YOUR PALS!
>
> I'm never going to understand why you and your friends seem to insist on proving to the world how JERKY you all can be by adding such wonders as a walrus penis to your site.
>
> That and the continued cigar smoking that occurs among your friends IS A CONSTANT SOURCE OF AGGRAVATION TO ME! Why won't you guys give yourselves a chance to grow up and show your fans that you can act normal? In the past I've asked your friends to help you be just a little more adult in your actions. IT HASN'T HELPED! I GUESS THEY DON'T REALLY CARE! Or maybe the truth is THEY are the real reason for the perverse actions seen on your site.
>
> Remember, you've only been married two weeks and already Jackie is walking around with a puzzled expression on her face. Just think what she's going to say when she knows you as long as I do. YOU'RE NOT MAKING IT EASY! DO THE RIGHT THING! Love ya, Dad.

chance to work with Barrymore again. After their first experience working together, he had nothing but praise for his costar. He said, "She's funny, smart, can get goofy at the drop of a hat, can listen to me and not yawn and [is] just plain old-fashioned cool as hell."[70]

Following *50 First Dates,* Sandler's next project is yet another change of pace. Much like *Punch-Drunk Love,* it was creatively rendered outside of the influence of Team Sandler and is being directed by a critically well-received director. Acclaimed filmmaker

Jackie Titone and Sandler wed in Malibu, California, in June 2003. With a successful career and a loving wife at his side, Sandler is confident his future will be very bright.

Wayne Wang, noted for the screen version of *The Joy Luck Club,* will direct the film called *Good Cook, Likes Music.* Sandler plays a man living with his mother in a trailer park who sends away for a mail-order bride. The young Asian woman arrives, and Sandler's character discovers she is a musical prodigy who changes his life. Also like *Punch-Drunk Love,* the film is not just a romantic comedy but has heavy dramatic overtones.

Into the Future

Once he completes *Good Cook, Likes Music,* Sandler is in the position to choose any project he wishes, and there are already several options. On July 13, 2003, he went into the studio to record his next comedy album. It is likely he will tour again, scheduling concert dates at colleges to promote the album when it is finished. He has stated in the past why the idea of a college concert tour appeals to him: "I like to know what's going on in an eighteen-year-old kid's mind. I like hanging out with twelve-year-old kids too, and hearing what they gotta say. . . . I want to be in touch with what's happening."[71]

Whatever Adam Sandler's next project may be, he has earned the respect of his loyal audience and the competitive industry he works in. He earned all this quicker than others have before him, but he earned it nonetheless.

It is extremely rare for any film star to have attained his high level of success and rarer still to maintain it over a long period of time. Adam Sandler has proved himself to be a versatile comedy performer who will undoubtedly be making audiences laugh for a very long time.

Notes

Chapter 1: Stan and Judy's Kid

1. Quoted in Julie Moran, *Entertainment Tonight Online,* June 7, 1999. www.etonline.com.
2. Quoted in Ben Stiller, *Interview,* December 1994, p. 104.
3. Quoted in Kate Meyers, "Adam Ribs," *Entertainment Weekly,* February 17, 1995, p. 26.
4. Quoted in Stiller, p. 107.
5. Quoted in Meredith Berkman, "Adam Sandler Is a Very Funny Guy," *Mademoiselle,* March 1995, p. 98.
6. Quoted in Berkman, "Adam Sandler Is a Very Funny Guy," p. 98.
7. Quoted in Berkman, "Adam Sandler Is a Very Funny Guy," p. 99.
8. Quoted in Karen S. Schneider, "Last Laugh," *People Weekly,* November 30, 1998, pp. 73–74.
9. Quoted in Schneider, "Last Laugh," p. 76.
10. Quoted in Jon Salem, *Adam Sandler Not Too Shabby!* New York: Scholastic, 1999, p. 11.
11. Quoted in David Poland, "The Wedding Singer Interview," *TNT Online,* 1998. http://adamsandler.jt.org.
12. Quoted in Jason Leivenberg, "Adam Sandler Unplugged," *Teen People,* December, 2002, p. 84.
13. Quoted in Stiller, p. 107.
14. Quoted in Jeanne Wolf, "The Wedding Singer Gets in Tune with His Mom, Drew Barrymore, and Chris Farley," *E! Entertainment,* 1998. http://eonline.com.

Chapter 2: They're All Gonna Laugh at You!

15. Quoted in Kevin Cook, "Checking In with Adam Sandler," *Playboy,* February 1999, p. 166.
16. Quoted in Schneider, "Last Laugh," p. 76.
17 Quoted in Kendall Hamilton and Yahlin Chang, "Oh, You Silly Boy," *Newsweek,* November 9, 1998, p. 69.
18. Quoted in Barry Koltnow, "Former *SNL* Comic Hopes to Reach a Wider Audience with New Golf Comedy," Knight/Ridder Tribune News Service, February 13, 1996.
19. Quoted in Schneider, "Last Laugh," p. 76.
20. Quoted in Bill Crawford, *Adam Sandler: America's Comedian.* New York: St. Martin's, 2000, p. 24.
21. Quoted in Dave Stern, *Adam Sandler, An Unauthorized Biography.* Los Angeles: Renaissance, 2000, p. 55.
22. Quoted in Betty Cortina, "Stop the Presses," *Entertainment Weekly,* June 18, 1999.
23. Quoted in Salem, *Adam Sandler Not Too Shabby!,* p. 28.
24. Quoted in *People Weekly,* "Adam Sandler, Laugh at Him, Laugh with Him: Either Way, He's Goofball King," December 28, 1998, p. 97.
25. Quoted in Stern, *Adam Sandler,* p. 60.
26. Quoted in Salem, *Adam Sandler Not Too Shabby!,* p. 26.
27. Quoted in Tom Shales and James Andrew Miller, *Live from New York.* Boston: Little, Brown, 2002, p. 363.

Chapter 3: Live from New York

28. Quoted in Shales and Miller, *Live from New York,* p. 363.
29. Quoted in Shales and Miller, *Live from New York,* p. 381.
30. Quoted in Rory Evans, "Seventeen Questions: Adam Sandler," *Seventeen,* April 1993, p. 92.
31. Quoted in Stern, *Adam Sandler,* p. 78.
32. Quoted in Stiller, p. 106.
33. Quoted in Stern, *Adam Sandler,* p. 92.
34. Quoted in Shales and Miller, *Live from New York,* p. 382.
35. Quoted in Schneider, "Last Laugh," p. 74.

36. Quoted in Jennifer Weiner, "Critics Scorn Adam Sandler's Dopey Humor, but It's a Hit with Audiences," Knight/Ridder Tribune News Service, February 22, 1996.
37. Quoted in Berkman, "Adam Sandler Is a Very Funny Guy," p. 98.
38. Quoted in Shales and Miller, *Live from New York,* p. 421.

Chapter 4: Team Sandler

39. Quoted in Stiller, p. 108.
40. Quoted in Koltnow, "Former *SNL* Comic Hopes to Reach a Wider Audience."
41. Quoted in Karen Hershenson, "*Saturday Night Live*'s Adam Sandler Is 'Happy' to Move into Films," Knight/Ridder Tribune News Service, February 15, 1996.
42. Quoted in Hamilton and Chang, "Oh, You Silly Boy," p. 69.
43. Quoted in Eric Layton, "The Big 80s," *Entertainment Today,* February 13, 1998.
44. Quoted in *America Online Chat,* February15, 1998. www.MTVarena.com.
45. Quoted in Crawford, *Adam Sandler,* p. 80.
46. Quoted in Crawford, *Adam Sandler,* p. 86.
47. Quoted in Stern, *Adam Sandler,* p. 175.
48. Quoted in Bob Thompson, "The Adam Family," *Toronto Sun,* February 8, 1998.
49. Quoted in Stern, *Adam Sandler,* p. 186.
50. Quoted in *Entertainment Tonight Online,* October 20, 1998. http://etonline.com.
51. Quoted in Steve Tilley, "Sandler's High Note," *Edmonton Sun,* February 4, 1998.
52. Quoted in *Entertainment Tonight Online.*

Chapter 5: Adam Sandler, Superstar

53. Quoted in Internet Movie Database, "Sandler Is Carreyed to the Top," November 10, 1998. www.imdb.com.
54. Quoted in Cortina, "Stop the Presses," p. 26.
55. Quoted in Cortina, "Stop the Presses," p. 26.

56. Quoted in Moran Entertainment Tonight, June 7, 1999. www.etonline.com.
57. Quoted in Moran Entertainment Tonight.
58. Quoted in Koltnow, "Former *SNL* Comic Hopes to Reach Wider Audience."
59. Quoted in News, Articles & Interviews. http://adamsandler.jt.org September 23, 1999, *MTV News.*
60. Quoted in Crawford, *Adam Sandler,* p. 145.
61. Quoted in Internet Movie Database, "Sandler's New Movie Trashes Town," July 10, 2001. www.imdb.com.
62. Quoted in Internet Movie Database, "Winona Fights the Pain," May 9, 2002. www.imdb.com.

Chapter 6: Changes

63. Quoted in *The Concert for New York City* liner notes, Columbia Music Video, 2001.
64. Quoted in Leivenberg, "Adam Sandler, Unplugged," p. 84.
65. Quoted in Brian D. Johnson, "Unhappy Gilmore: What Happens When a Hollywood Star and an Iconoclast Director Join Forces," *Maclean's,* October 14, 2002, p. 84.
66. Quoted in Brian M. Raftery, "Stretch Marks," *Entertainment Weekly,* October 25, 2002, p. 8.
67. Quoted in Internet Movie Database, "Adam Sandler's Fiancée Problems," June 13, 2002. www.imdb.com.
68. Quoted in *People Weekly,* "The Wedding Zinger," July 7, 2003, p. 117.
69. Quoted in *People Weekly,* "The Wedding Zinger," p. 117.
70. Quoted in *America Online Chat.*
71. Quoted in Internet Movie Database, "Sandler's College Tour," June 28, 2002. www.imdb.com.

Important Dates in the Life of Adam Sandler

1966
Adam Richard Sandler is born in Brooklyn, New York, on September 9.

1972
The Sandler family moves to Manchester, New Hampshire, where Adam attends public school.

1984
Goes onstage to perform comedy in Boston's Stitches Comedy Club at brother's urging. Enters NYU that fall on a theater scholarship.

1987
Makes TV debut on *The Cosby Show.* Regular on MTV's *Remote Control.*

1988
Becomes semiregular as Smitty on *The Cosby Show.*

1989
Appears in his first film, *Going Overboard.*

1990
Gets top spot at Comic Strip Live in New York. Begins dating Margaret Ruden. Moves briefly to Los Angeles to try the comedy clubs there. Auditions for *Saturday Night Live* and is hired as writer.

1991
Earns his fine arts degree from NYU. Joins cast of *SNL* as featured player. Plays Dink in the film *Shakes the Clown.*

1993

Appears in *Coneheads* movie. *They're All Gonna Laugh at You!* released and goes triple platinum. Becomes full cast member in *SNL's* 1993–1994 season.

1994

On screen in the films *Mixed Nuts* and *Airheads.*

1995

Billy Madison premieres in theaters. Leaves *SNL.* "The Chanukah Song" released as single and becomes a holiday standard on Top 40 radio stations. Breaks up with girlfriend Margaret Ruden.

1996

Happy Gilmore and *Bulletproof* released. *What the Hell Happened to Me?* CD released.

1997

Least successful CD, *What's Your Name?,* released but still sells more than a million copies. Chris Farley dies.

1998

The Wedding Singer released and earns good reviews. *The Waterboy* released and breaks box-office records. Begins dating Jackie Titone.

1999

Big Daddy released. Animated short "The Peeper" premieres on the Internet to promote *Stan and Judy's Kid.*

2000

Little Nicky released to disappointing box office.

2001

Following the tragedy of September 11, appears at *America: A Tribute to Heroes* and *The Concert for New York City.*

2002

Mr. Deeds released and is a box-office success. Releases animated film *Eight Crazy Nights.* Receives Golden Globe nomination for *Punch-Drunk Love.* Announces engagement to Jackie Titone.

2003

Anger Management, filmed in post–September 11 New York with Jack Nicholson, is released and is another box-office blockbuster. Films *50 First Dates* with Drew Barrymore. Marries girlfriend Jackie Titone on June 22. Begins recording his next album.

For Further Reading

Books

Bill Crawford, *Adam Sandler: America's Comedian.* New York: St. Martin, 2000. Good biography with up-to-date information and categorized subjects. Later chapter about censorship is very explicit.

Jon Salem, *Adam Sandler Not Too Shabby!* New York: Scholastic, 1999. Juvenile biography of Sandler written with a slant toward younger readers in both style and content.

Tom Shales and James Andrew Miller, *Live from New York.* Boston: Little, Brown, 2002. Well-written oral biography of the metamorphosis of *Saturday Night Live,* with many anecdotes from the participants of the show up to the present day. Includes interviews with virtually every cast member and writer, including Sandler. A must-read for any fan of the show.

Dave Stern, *Adam Sandler, An Unauthorized Biography.* Los Angeles: Renaissance, 2000. Well-researched biography with impressive background information and a photo section with color pictures. Includes an extensive bibliography.

Periodicals

Jess Cagle, "Sandler, Seriously," *Time,* October 21, 2002.

Kendall Hamilton and Yahlin Chang, "Oh, You Silly Boy," *Newsweek,* November 9, 1998.

Kate Meyers, "Adam Ribs," *Entertainment Weekly,* February 17, 1995.

People Weekly, "The Wedding Zinger," July 7, 2003.

Karen S. Schneider, "Last Laugh," *People Weekly,* November 30, 1998.

Ben Stiller, *Interview,* December 1994.

Websites

The Adam Sandler Experience (http://adamsandler.jt.org). This site boasts that it is the oldest fan-based Sandler website on the Internet, and as such, it is extremely impressive. There are contests for fans of Sandler trivia, audio downloads from films and CDs, interviews, and links to other fan sites.

Adam Sandler's Official Website (www.adamsandler.com). Sandler's website includes links to his movie websites, updates on his projects, many pictures of Happy Madison employees on location and in the office, video downloads from his CDs, downloadable video messages from Sandler updated monthly, and contests involving his dog, Meatball. There are also recent and archived letters from his father and pictures from his wedding.

Internet Movie Database (www.imdb.com). Includes a biography of Sandler as well as pictures, links to other websites, details of his films, and daily updates of his projects.

***Saturday Night Live* Website** (http://snl.jt.org). Anyone seeking any information on the history of *Saturday Night Live* will find it here. Every episode, every host, every musical guest, every sketch, and every character are meticulously categorized. Even lists everyone who ever opened the show with the famous line. Important to read home page instructions before continuing, otherwise it can be very confusing.

Works Consulted

Book

Ted Okuda and James Neibaur, *Jerry Lewis Films*. North Carolina: McFarland, 1995. This comprehensive and detailed account of the comedian's film career includes photos from every film and annotations by Lewis himself.

Periodicals

Mae Anderson, "All About Adam," *Adweek*, August 5, 2002.

Chuck Arnold, "Chatter," *People Weekly*, March 9, 1998.

———, "Chatter," *People Weekly*, November 23, 1998.

———, "Chatter," *People Weekly*, December 28, 1998.

Deborah Baer, "Adam Sandler: Come On, You Just Have to Love a Multimillionaire Movie Star Who Can Get Away with Wearing Sweatpants," *CosmoGIRL!*, August 2002.

Meredith Berkman, "Adam Sandler Is a Very Funny Guy," *Mademoiselle*, March 1995.

Mark Cetner, "Adam Sandler's Secret Life," *National Enquirer*, July 27, 1999.

Kevin Cook, "Checking In with Adam Sandler," *Playboy*, February 1999.

Betty Cortina, "Stop the Presses," *Entertainment Weekly*, June 18, 1999.

Current Biography Yearbook, H.W. Wilson, New York 1998.

Entertainment Weekly, "Big Trouble," July 9, 1999.

Rory Evans, "Seventeen Questions: Adam Sandler," *Seventeen*, April 1993.

Nancy Gondo, "Comedian Exhibits Dramatic Range," *Daily Variety,* January 8, 2003.

Dana Harris, "Sandler Will Pucker Up for 'Kisses,'" *Daily Variety,* December 9, 2002.

Karen Hershenson, "*Saturday Night Live's* Adam Sandler Is 'Happy' to Move into Films," Knight/Ridder Tribune News Service, February 15, 1996.

Chris Hewitt, "*Eight Crazy Nights* Review," Knight/Ridder Tribune News Service, November 26, 2002.

———, "*Mr. Deeds* Review," Knight/Ridder Tribune News Service, June 26, 2002.

Christopher Kelly, "Rob Schneider and Adam Sandler Flicks Have 'Animal' Magnetism," Knight/Ridder Tribune News Service, June 8, 2001.

Barry Koltnow, "Former *SNL* Comic Hopes to Reach a Wider Audience with New Golf Comedy," Knight/Ridder Tribune News Service, February 13, 1996.

———, "Sandler Fans Respond in Crayon," *Orange County Register,* July 8, 2002.

Brian D. Johnson, "Unhappy Gilmore: What Happens When a Hollywood Star and an Iconoclast Director Join Forces," *Maclean's*, October 14, 2002.

Tricia Johnson, "Gimme Shelter," *Entertainment Weekly,* April 20, 2001.

Eric Layton, "The Big 80s," *Entertainment Today,* February 13, 1998.

Jason Leivenberg, "Adam Sandler, Unplugged," *Teen People,* December 2002.

Moira MacDonald, "Paul Thomas Anderson Is Now Punch-Drunk over Comedy," *Seattle Times,* October 15, 2002.

Jack Matthews, "Why 'Mr. Deeds' Went to Town and 'Little Nicky' Didn't," *New York Daily News,* July 2, 2002.

Kate Meyers, "Adam Sandler, Face to Watch," *Entertainment Weekly,* September 11, 1993.

Tiarra Mukherjee, "Lights FM," *Entertainment Weekly,* January 19, 1996.

People Weekly, "Adam Sandler, Laugh at Him, Laugh with Him: Either Way, He's a Goofball King," December 28, 1998.

Brian M. Raftery, "Stretch Marks," *Entertainment Weekly,* October 25, 2002.

Steve Rushin, "The Hits Keep Coming," *Sports Illustrated,* November 30, 1998.

Dan Snierson, "4 Adam Sandler," *Entertainment Weekly,* December 25, 1998.

Bob Thompson, "The Adam Family," *Toronto Sun,* February 8, 1998.

Steve Tilley, "Sandler's High Note" *Edmonton Sun,* February 4, 1998.

Variety, "Sandler/Nicholson Team Official," December 24, 2001.

Bruce Vilanch, "A Kiss Is Just a Kiss," *Advocate,* December 7, 1999.

Jennifer Weiner, "Critics Scorn Adam Sandler's Dopey Humor, but It's a Hit with Audiences," Knight/Ridder Tribune News Service, February 22, 1996.

Internet Sources

Biography Resource Center, "Comedian Adam Sandler Breaks Record for Highest First Week Sales with New Warner Bros. CD, 'Stan and Judy's Kid,'" September 30, 1999. http://galegroup.com.

Internet Movie Database, "Adam Sandler's Fiancée Problems," June 13, 2002. www.imdb.com.

———, "Sandler Is Carried to the Top," November 10, 1998. www.imdb.com.

———, "Sandler's College Tour," June 28, 2002. www.imdb.com.

———, "Sandler's New Movie Trashes Town," July 10, 2001. www.imdb.com.

———, "Winona Fights the Pain," May 9, 2002. www.imdb.com.

Julie Moran, Entertainment Tonight, June 7, 1999. www.etonline.com.

David Poland, "The Wedding Singer Interview," TNT Online. http://adamsandler.jt.org.

Jeanne Wolf, "The Wedding Singer Gets in Tune with His Mom, Drew Barrymore, and Chris Farley," *E! Entertainment.* www.eonline.com.

Albums

Adam Sandler, *Stan and Judy's Kid.* Warner Brothers, 1999.

———, *They're All Gonna Laugh at You!* Warner Brothers, 1993.

———, *What the Hell Happened to Me?* Warner Brothers, 1996.

———, *What's Your Name?* Warner Brothers, 1997.

DVDs

The Concert For New York City, Columbia Music Video, 2001.

Going Overboard, Trimark Home Video, 1989.

Index

Picture Credits

Cover: © Getty Images
© Stephane Cardinale/Corbis, 9
© Mitchell Gerber/CORBIS, 21, 34
© Lynn Goldsmith/CORBIS, 38
© Nick Goossen/AdamSandler.com/WireImage.com, 90
© Steve Granitz/WireImage.com, 57, 68
© Robert Holmes/CORBIS, 27
© Hulton-Deutsch Collection/CORBIS, 11
© Kevin Kane/WireImage.com, 41
© Patti Ouderkirk/WireImage.com, 15
© Photofest, 17, 45, 46, 49, 52, 55, 60, 63, 67, 70, 74, 76, 83, 84, 87
© Chris Pizzello/WireImage.com, 24
© John Springer Collection/CORBIS, 9
© Denise Truscello/WireImage.com, 31
© Theo Wargo/WireImage.com, 81
© Mychal Watts/WireImage.com, 28

About the Author

Dwayne Epstein was born in Brooklyn, New York, and grew up in Southern California. His first professional writing credit was in 1982, writing film reviews and year-end analysis of popular culture.

Nationally, he has been a regular contributor to several film magazines since 1996. Internationally, he contributed to Bill Krohn's *Serious Pleasures* in 1997, which saw publication in Europe. Epstein has had several children's books published since 2000 and is currently writing a biography of actor Lee Marvin. He lives in Long Beach, California, with his girlfriend, Barbara, and too many books on movie history.